Ron Hull
3-4-80

THE CASE FOR BIBLICAL CHRISTIANITY

THE CASE FOR BIBLICAL CHRISTIANITY

EDWARD JOHN CARNELL

edited by

RONALD H. NASH

WILLIAM B. EERDMANS PUBLISHING COMPANY
GRAND RAPIDS, MICHIGAN

Printed in the United States of America

Library of Congress Catalog Card Number: 68-20584

Grateful acknowledgment is given to the following journals and publishers for their assistance and for their permission to reprint the material used in this book.

The Christian Century, Kyle Haselden, editor

Christianity Today, Carl F. H. Henry, editor

Wm. B. Eerdmans Publishing Company

Encounter, Calvin L. Porter, editor

Eternity, Russell T. Hitt, editor

His, Paul Frome, editor

The Journal of Bible and Religion, Harry M. Buck, Jr., editor

The Macmillan Company

Religion in Life, published by The Abingdon Press

Charles Scribner's Sons

The Westminster Press

Editor's Preface

Edward John Carnell will be remembered as one of the more prolific and articulate apologists for biblical Christianity in our generation. His untimely death at the age of 47 in April of 1967 ended the ministry of a man generally acknowledged to be one of conservative Christianity's brightest scholars. His many books and articles revealed a well-disciplined mind, steeped deeply in classical and contemporary philosophy and theology. He was a rare phenomenon in twentieth-century theology—an orthodox theologian who was eager to engage in both debate and dialogue with non-conservatives and a man who displayed none of the bitterness and rancor of many fundamentalists.

This is Professor Carnell's last book. When he died, he left behind a legacy of eight books, a seminary whose fortunes he had guided for five of his nineteen years on its faculty, and a host of pastors and Christian leaders who had learned from him that one did not have to be defensive about accepting the tenets of orthodox Christianity in the twentieth century. But Carnell also left behind more than a score of articles written for various journals and books over a period of some twenty years. Because I was familiar with most of these articles, I knew that many merited republication. This anthology is the fruit of that conviction.

This collection of essays has, I believe, many things to recommend it. It gives the Christian community ready access to many of the splendid articles that Carnell wrote during his career, articles that would otherwise have remained buried deep within stacks of dusty, unbound periodicals. The pastor, theologian, and philosopher will find, as always in Carnell's writings, thoughtful, stimulating, and often provocative essays on theology, philosophy of religion, ethics, ecumenism, fundamentalism, separatism, and other topics of contemporary interest.

Most of the major concerns of Carnell's thought are represented in this collection. For example, his first love was apologetics, the philosophical defense of the Christian Faith. His very first book, *An Introduction to Christian Apologetics* (1948), set the stage for much of his later work, even though he admittedly modified some of the positions he took in this early writing. In *Christian Apologetics,* Carnell offered a defense of biblical Christianity in terms of a rationalistic and idealistic world view. Making his appeal primarily to the law of non-contradiction and secondarily to the facts of science and history, Carnell argued that Christianity provides the believer with a rational world view that is internally self-consistent and that fits the facts of science and history. In his *Philosophy of the Christian Religion* (1952), he appealed not so much to logic as to axiology, the science of values. His third book on apologetics, *Christian Commitment* (1957), revealed a growing indebtedness to the thought of the nineteenth-century Christian philosopher, Søren Kierkegaard. Carnell now supplemented his earlier appeals to logic and value with an apologetic based upon what he called "the third method of knowing" and "the judicial sentiment."*

Carnell continued to regard *Christian Commitment* as his best book and he remained disappointed that it never received the hearing and support accorded to most of his other books. Chapter Six in this volume includes selections from *Christian Commitment* which illustrate the apologetic he sought to develop on the basis of his third method of knowing. Carnell recognized that apologetics has its limitations. It cannot bring a man to Christ; only the preaching of the gospel can do this. However, apologetics is a useful and sometimes necessary tool in removing obstacles that come between the sinner and Christ.

Another obstacle that can hinder a man's quest for God is spurious theology. This volume contains several articles in which Carnell discusses important aspects of Christian theology, e.g., the virgin birth, the atonement, the Christian ethic. It also contains articles in which Carnell criticizes two major alternatives to orthodox Christianity, religious liberalism and neo-orthodoxy. Liberalism tried to supplant orthodoxy with a Pelagian view of man that substituted human effort for divine grace and a pantheistic view of God that blurred the distinction between Creator and creature. Both liberalism and neo-orthodoxy undermined the authority of the Bible; both positions

*However, Carnell's first references to "the third method of knowing" and "the third locus of truth" appear in his *Philosophy of the Christian Religion.*

reduced Christianity to a kind of religious subjectivism which left man without any objective guide in his search for God. Chapter Five, "Faith and Reason," expresses Carnell's conviction that theological positions must be judged on the adequacy of their epistemology. Carnell's critique of liberalism and neo-orthodoxy in this chapter is primarily an attack on their subjectivistic, non-propositional view of revelation and their inadequate view of the relation between faith and reason. Carnell raises a similar objection to Reinhold Niebuhr's thought in Chapter Nine ("Reinhold Niebuhr's Criteria of Verification").

Mention of Niebuhr brings us to another major concern in Carnell's writings. Carnell wrote one of his doctoral dissertations on Niebuhr and much of this was incorporated in his early work, *The Theology of Reinhold Niebuhr* (1951). In addition to Chapter Nine, already mentioned, Chapters Seven and Eight provide us with a contrast between Niebuhr and Billy Graham and with a study of Niebuhr's view of Scripture. With respect to Chapter Seven ("On Reinhold Niebuhr and Billy Graham"), one warning is necessary. The chapter contains two articles occasioned by Niebuhr's criticisms of Graham's approach to evangelism and, in particular, by Niebuhr's opposition to Graham's New York City campaign in the mid-1950's. The reader therefore should keep in mind the limited purposes of the articles. They are included here because they contain some important aspects of Dr. Carnell's teaching, especially with reference to the relationship between theology and churchmanship.

While Carnell was forced occasionally to engage in polemics, he never lost his concern for Christian unity. Chapters One ("Christian Fellowship and the Unity of the Church"), Two ("The Nature of the Unity We Seek"), and Three ("Conservatives and Liberals Do Not Need Each Other") exhibit different aspects of this concern; they also make clear his refusal to accept unity on terms that would force the church in the direction of doctrinal inclusivism. Incidentally, another warning is needed, this time in connection with Chapter Three. This essay was originally published in *Christianity Today* as a companion to an article that maintained that conservatives and liberals *do* need each other. There is reason to believe Carnell wrote this at the express request of the editor of *Christianity Today* as a reply to the other article. Undoubtedly, in another context and at another time, Carnell might have been concerned to develop other aspects of this topic.

Carnell is also known for his attempts to correct certain excesses within Protestant orthodoxy. He admitted that when he graduated from seminary, he had stars in his eyes. The imperfections of orthodoxy were not yet visible to him. But he soon came to see that while orthodoxy did possess the truth of God, it carried that truth in earthen vessels. The trouble, Carnell insisted, was not with orthodoxy's theology; the difficulty lay in the attitudes, dispositions, and practices of orthodox Christians. As he listed them in the last chapter of his *The Case for Orthodox Theology* (1959)*, these included "the quest for negative status, the elevation of minor issues to a place of major importance, the use of social mores as a norm of virtue, the toleration of one's own prejudice but not the prejudice of others, the confusion of the church with a denomination, and the avoidance of prophetic scrutiny by using the Word of God as an instrument of security but not self-criticism." Carnell became increasingly dismayed with the hyper-separatists within orthodoxy who, often prompted by apparently selfish motives, produced schism after schism in the church. Orthodoxy's proneness to theological nit-picking, its frequent indifference to social problems, and its oft-recurring anti-intellectualism were hindrances to conservatism's attempt to mediate God's truth to modern man. However, in spite of its problems, Carnell continued to defend orthodoxy; it still had much more to offer the world than liberalism — it had the gospel! As Carnell put it, "Despite its anachronisms and inconsistencies...orthodoxy remains a stronghold of biblical Christianity. It puts first things first. It preaches that 'without the shedding of blood there is no forgiveness of sins' . . . . If the church fails to tell sinners how to be saved, of what final value is anything else that is said?" By now it is a familiar story how many extremists within the fundamentalist camp turned on Carnell. However, it should be made clear that most of their criticisms were ill-founded. Those fundamentalists who incorrectly accused Carnell of abandoning the evangelical view of the Scriptures should note that throughout the essays in this volume, he maintains a high view of the Bible and its inspiration. To the last, he continued to criticize the representatives of neo-orthodoxy for abandoning a propositional view of revelation. Many conservatives who were less than pleased with Carnell's *Case for Orthodox Theology* must have put the book away before they came to his closing chapter. That chapter with its honest appraisal of orthodoxy is reprinted

*Reprinted in this volume as Chapter Fifteen.

along with Carnell's evaluation of the other two volumes in the Westminster Trilogy.

Another essay that deals with fundamentalism, "Orthodoxy: Cultic vs. Classical" (Chapter Four) marked an important stage in the development of Carnell's thought. Those fundamentalist critics who never completely understood his opposition to separatism will find his reasons spelled out here in great detail.

There are several other articles included in this volume but we shall let them speak for themselves. May I add just a word to those careful readers who will perhaps detect a few inconsistencies in these articles. One should remember that they were written over a period of twenty years, and only stagnant waters never change. Obviously Carnell's thought developed and underwent some alterations during these years. However, in no case did he deviate from the doctrinal tenets of orthodox theology.

It is still too early to evaluate the work of Edward John Carnell. Perhaps the best appraisal we can give now is a *paraphrase* of an evaluation he once wrote about Billy Graham.

> The issue, it seems to me, is not whether Edward John Carnell was always biblically consistent in his teaching. Each of us unconsciously cultivates some heresy or other. The issue is whether Edward John Carnell was morally uneasy about his inability to be biblically consistent. As long as he was willing to know the right and be transformed by it, the fundamentalist can ask for nothing more. And the reason he can ask for nothing more is that nothing more can be asked of the fundamentalist.

I wish to acknowledge my indebtedness to all the publishers and editors who graciously consented to permit material from their books and journals to be reprinted. My colleague, Dr. Roy Butler, and Dr. David Allan Hubbard, President of Fuller Theological Seminary, offered many helpful suggestions. I wish also to thank Dr. William S. Sailer of The Evangelical Congregational School of Theology and Dr. Joe E. Barnhart of North Texas State University for their assistance on the bibliography.

RONALD H. NASH
Department of Philosophy and Religion
Western Kentucky University

Contents

CHAPTER ONE

Christian Fellowship and the Unity of the Church

When the mourners gathered at the grave of Lazarus, they experienced perfect unity. Jesus Himself was the rallying point for fellowship, doctrine, and form: *fellowship* because the mourners were bound by cords of love; *doctrine* because the teaching of the Lord was normative; and *form* because the will of the Lord became the will of the group. The mourners were all of one mind.

The church remained united after Jesus ascended to heaven and questions of doctrine and form had to be settled by the apostolic college. These questions did not disrupt the unity because they were placed at the service of the fellowship. The believers knew that if they failed to love one another, their profession in doctrine and form would profit nothing.

When great numbers were added to the church, this ideal was not surrendered. The believers were together in the temple; they were together from house to house.

It was not long, however, before believers began to boast that they were of Paul, Apollos, and Cephas. Party spirit corrupted the purity of the fellowship. The tragedy of a divided church is almost as old as the joy of a united church. Party spirit has plagued the fellowship from the middle of the apostolic age until now. The verdict of history is clear.

I

The Roman Catholic Church played a leading role in guiding believers from the warmth of Pentecost to a time when believers not only faced the wrath of the empire and a spawn of heresies,

Originally published in Edward John Carnell's *The Kingdom of Love and the Pride of Life* (Grand Rapids, Eerdmans, 1961), pp. 110-121. Reprinted by permission.

but when they could look neither to Jerusalem as the center of worship nor to the collective wisdom of the living apostles. A magnificent effort was put forth, and with many lasting benefits.

But at least one capital mistake was made. The Roman Church began to crystallize its traditions before the epistles of Paul had been thoroughly circulated and studied.[1] As a result, the full import of justification by faith was not comprehended. A Roman believer could never rest in the finished work of Christ; he could lose his salvation at any time by committing a mortal sin. A spirit of legalism sullied the biblical concept of grace. This spirit did much to obscure the fellowship, for love and fear are moral opposites.

When the Roman Church faced the spawn of heresies, it was so anxious to preserve internal unity that it lodged the *charisma veritatis* in the bishop, rather than in the original apostolic college. The church was then conceived as the continued incarnation of Christ. Christ was present in the person of ecclesiastical officers.

With the triumph of form, the Roman bishops dealt harshly with prophets who tried to call the church back to the teachings of the original apostolic college. Rome believed then, as it does now, that no man is rightly joined to Christ unless he is rightly joined to his bishop. This means that justification is decided by a believer's relation to an institution, rather than by personal confrontation with Christ.

Luther repented of sin; he received Jesus as Lord and Saviour; and he believed all that was spoken by the prophets and apostles. But these virtues fell short of Roman requirements. An offense against the form of the church was the same as an offense against fellowship and doctrine.

Rather than gently correcting Luther, Rome excommunicated him. The great schism in Western Christendom traces as much to Roman intransigence as it does to Luther's own sense of individualism. No real opportunity was given to investigate the relation between fellowship, doctrine, and form.

When Luther and his congregation sang *A Mighty Fortress Is Our God*, one of the great moments in the life of the church was realized. Luther succeeded in liberating the fellowship from the confines of form. And by this liberation he opened the way for the purifying of doctrine.

[1] See Thomas F. Torrance, *The Doctrine of Grace in the Apostolic Fathers* (Grand Rapids, Eerdmans, 1959).

II

In an alarmingly short time, however, Lutheranism converted to an institution which defined faith as assent to right doctrine, and which granted the prince many of the rights enjoyed by the Roman bishop. Lutherans were no more charitable to dissenters than Roman Catholics were. An Anabaptist could repent of sin; he could receive Jesus as Lord and Saviour; and he could believe all that was spoken by the prophets and apostles. But these virtues fell short of Lutheran requirements. Unless a penitent affirmed, according to the Wittenberg Concord, "that with the bread and wine are truly and substantially present, offered, and received the body and blood of Christ," he was not part of the fellowship.

The internal struggles in Lutheranism, together with the historic tendency of Lutherans to go it alone, can only be accounted for on the assumption that doctrine and form rank higher than fellowship.

The disturbing part of Lutheran particularity is the fact that insufficient allowance is made for either the subtle scholastic arguments that undergird the Lutheran view of the eucharist, or the inability of believers in other traditions to feel the force of such arguments.

III

Calvin performed the spectacular feat of delivering the church from state control.[2] His penetration of divine grace left little place for human complacency. The *Institutes* forms the finest treatise in Protestant theology. Aesthetic proportion and personal piety blend with a scholar's command of Scripture.

But when Calvinism converted to a theological system, it turned out that the "elect of God" were those who accepted the distinctive teachings of John Calvin. Once again, doctrine and form ranked higher than fellowship. An Arminian could repent of sin; he could receive Jesus as Lord and Saviour; and he could believe all that was spoken by the prophets and apostles. But these virtues fell short of Calvinistic requirements. Unless a believer accepted the doctrine of irresistible grace, he was not a part of the fellowship.

Calvinism did not create an institution as such, but it imitated Catholicism and Lutheranism by drawing up a

[2] See Emil Brunner, *The Misunderstanding of the Church* (Philadelphia, Westminster, 1953).

confession that would serve as a touchstone of correct doctrine, and thus of fit fellowship. But this confession, like those it imitated, was never ratified by the church universal.

Calvinism had no excuse for freezing theological inquiry at the level of the *Institutes*. A careful examination of that document will show that Calvin himself, despite his great genius, failed to harmonize the divine decrees with human responsibility. Now, if a theology is defective at such a critical point, how can it serve as a norm of fellowship?

IV

The British fear of innovation insulated Anglicanism from the more radical by-products of the Reformation. Gradually a way was opened for high, medium, and low expression of liturgy within the one church form.

Outsiders may think that Anglicanism has reverted to the age of the judges, where each man does what is right in his own eyes. But more discriminating minds will perceive that Anglicanism is a majestic, if not altogether unique, effort to subordinate form to fellowship. An Englishman is not much of a gentleman if he is dishonest, and especially when he worships God. Decent decorum requires, therefore, that full allowance be made for the differences in temperament that exist within the various strata of society. By this expedient, greater liberty in the Spirit is encouraged. Some Christians prefer a minimum of ritual, while others feel impoverished unless the ritual is ancient and elaborate.

But the British fear of innovation has all too often been federated with a subtle defense of British interests. Although Anglicanism defends the church universal in its articles of faith, in the real business of daily life it reserves patronage and power for Anglicans.

The religious wars in England trace, in great part, to the intransigence of the established church. Dissenters could repent of sin; they could receive Jesus as Lord and Saviour; and they could believe all that was spoken by the prophets and apostles. But these virtues fell short of Anglican requirements. Unless a believer supported the traditions of the established church, he was not part of the fellowship.

V

When the Puritans, Scotch Presbyterians, and Methodists succeeded in overturning the papacy, the crown, and the established church, the Christian community was given fresh opportunities to make the fellowship as wide as Christ intended it. But each group was too occupied with improving its own position to take creative leadership in this higher question.

The Puritans restored the classical standards in theology. They composed a body of literature which was a credit to that or any other day. No major topic in the theological encyclopedia was left unexplored.

But the Puritans (with notable exceptions) tended to be parochial in outlook, for they never succeeded in transcending the limitations of Calvinism. They used the distinctive elements in this theology as a measure of correct doctrine, and thus of fit fellowship. They envisioned a theocracy reserved for the "elect."

Scotch Presbyterians drank the full cup of Reformation heroism. They followed Knox in putting their feet on the necks of kings and queens, while bowing in the dust before Almighty God.

But Scotch Presbyterians impaired the fellowship by insisting that presbyterian polity was the only biblical polity. Once again, fit fellowship was decided by correct doctrine and form. Moreover, Scotch Presbyterians, like many Lutherans, have tended to link the interests of the church with the interests of race and soil.

Methodists successfully rebuked Anglican formalism by returning to the biblical emphasis on personal holiness. Although Methodism did little to advance the dialogue in classical theology, it did write an inspiring chapter in frontier evangelism. The gospel was preached with unexampled power and conviction. A lively hope was brought to the working classes.

But many Methodists were not satisfied with this. They used the doctrine of personal holiness as a denominational status symbol, and thus as a reason for separating from the church universal. And when Methodists resisted the cultic tendency, they imitated Anglicanism by drawing up an episcopal polity that reserves patronage and power for Methodists. And since Methodist polity is untempered by the British symbols of the crown and the British gift of understatement, it is often more rigid and bureaucratic than Anglicanism.

VI

Baptists and Congregationalists have hit the trail of independence. They say that the New Testament refers to the local congregation as a church. The evidence is not conclusive, of course, but it is sufficient to encourage the conviction that every local congregation is a self-contained unit. All other associations are voluntary expedients aimed at encouraging richer fellowship among congregations. The Bible is elevated above human creeds, and each believer enjoys liberty of conscience as a priest of God.

With this catalogue of virtues to draw on, independent churches ought to enjoy ideal conditions for the improvement of Christian fellowship. But there is often a wide gap between theory and practice.

The woes of Baptists and Congregationalists are easy to recount. As life in the communion becomes more involved, there is a gradual encroachment upon the liberty of the local congregation. The "voluntary associations" eventually assume the form of an institution. In the end, loyalty to Christ is equated with loyalty to the denomination. It is ironic, therefore, that local Baptist and Congregational churches often have less liberty than congregations under the parish system.[3]

VII

The separatist settles things by organizing a church of which he himself is the head. His policies are crudely dictatorial, yet he sometimes encourages levels of fellowship that the historic denominations frown on. The diversity of spiritual gifts is accepted without embarrassment, and a genuine effort is made to encourage lay participation.

But the way of the separatist is seldom a happy one. Being out of fellowship with both the church universal and the wisdom of the ages, the separatist is prey to novelty and enthusiasm. He cannot discern shades of better and worse in his own theology; he has no biblical answer to anarchy. Moreover, he is inflated with a feeling of personal superiority. Rather than trying to heal existing divisions in the church, he is busy creating new ones.

VIII

Many believers in the modern church are searching for a happier way to blend fellowship, doctrine, and form. They

[3] Paul M. Harrison says it is high time that Baptists develop a genuine representational system of government. See *Authority and Power in the Free Church Tradition* (Princeton).

are gathering for friendly, exploratory conversation. This is a genuinely hopeful sign.

Still, the effort only points up the paradox of our witness as Christians. Individual believers may be willing to surrender institutional status, but the institution itself, with its vested interests and tangled bureaucracy, goes right on defending the status quo. In one room there is conversation about enlarging the fellowship, while down the hall committees are busy devising new ways to perpetuate the patronage and power of the institution.

What can be done about this paradox? Well, for one thing we can *acknowledge* the paradox. Since the church falls short of the ideals set down in Scripture, we may just as well come right out and admit it.[4] Nothing will be gained either by wringing our hands in despair, or by dreaming of utopian conditions that overlook the limits that original sin places on history. With all our lofty theories of the church, the grim fact remains that the institution is more concerned with jurisdiction than it is with fellowship. Money must be handled and property titled. As vested interests evolve, new power blocs are formed to protect them.

If the church were to acknowledge its imperfection, a climate of honesty might be created in which believers could wait on the Holy Spirit to show them happier ways to blend fellowship, doctrine, and form.

IX

There is little reason to believe that the denominations will ever succeed in drawing up a confession that is acceptable to all parties. Confessions not only mirror the times, but they have a disturbing way of converting to final, inspired documents. If a theologian proposes that a confession be brought into more perfect harmony with Scripture, he is charged with departing from the faith once for all delivered to the saints.

The Roman Catholic Church forthrightly announces that its confessions are infallible. But this only adds to the paradox of our witness as Christians. When Rome summoned the Council of Trent in the pressure of the Counter-Reformation, it not only acted with haste, but it drew up a creed that was defined against the excesses of sixteenth-century Lutheranism.

[4] See Leslie Newbigin, *The Household of God* (New York, Friendship, 1954).

But how can Rome improve upon a creed that has been declared infallible?

X

The modern church is trying to shrink the paradox by merging denominations of like heritage. Such mergers, when undertaken with proper ends in view, should by all means be encouraged. If Christians agree on doctrine, they should learn to agree on form. Denominational reduplication not only hinders the fellowship, but it is an inexcusable waste of money and talent.

But merger is not the whole answer. For one thing, it may serve as a substitute for individual responsibility. Shrinking the number of denominations is no blessing *per se*. Christ prayed for unity, but not for organizational unity. He prayed that His followers might be one, even as the Father and the Son are one. This implies a *vital* unity, and vital unity implies fellowship. Thus, if organizational merger detracts Christians from their obligation to love one another, it is a hindrance to unity, not an encouragement.

Moreover, the major denominations grew out of a sincere effort to honor the teachings of Scripture. Scripture does not claim to give a finished system. When the Apostle Paul says, "I know in part," he speaks for the whole church.

It is only natural, therefore, that theologians will disagree on questions such as polity, the eucharist, the subjects and modes of baptism, predestination, and degrees of sanctification. And such disagreements are bound to be reflected in the forms that the Christian community assumes when it enters history. We should not be ashamed of our theological differences. They are signs that we are taking the work of exegesis seriously. Furthermore, a genuine Christian fellowship can exist *within* the framework of denominational plurality. Love can hurdle existing barriers.

Roman Catholicism insists that it is the only true church, but its claims are refuted by the plain facts of history. Whether Rome cares to acknowledge it or not, God has true believers in *every* professing church. All we can do is stand back and rejoice at the manifold operations of divine grace. Whenever there are genuine signs of faith and repentance, we must presume that the gospel is at work. And having made this admission, we then should try to find some way to bring all Christians into fellowship.

Roman Catholicism is in an awkward position. Whenever

it says it is willing to hold conversation with "separated brethren," it simultaneously affirms and denies that there is no salvation outside the church.

XI

Despairing of a confessional route to unity, many are proposing that we unite around a least common denominator. This denominator will be so all-inclusive that no believer will be excluded from the fellowship.

The expedient is attractive, but it has its price. Once we become indifferent to right doctrine, it will not be long before we shall also become indifferent to fit fellowship; for the two go together. Saving faith does not take place in a vacuum. It is an act that grows out of a vital response to the gospel, and the gospel is based on specific redemptive events. If we disparage these events, we surrender the normative elements in the Christian religion.

XII

Many obstacles stand in the way of Christian brotherhood. But if we sincerely believe in the communion of the saints, we must continue to strive for more perfect ways to express this brotherhood in history. If God has ordained that doctrine and form should be servants of the fellowship, then we should see that God's will is done on earth as it is in heaven. Whatever impedes the fellowship must be brought under critical scrutiny.

Some help may be found by returning to the grave of Lazarus. When Jesus wept, the mourners were so perfectly controlled by the Holy Spirit that they were delivered from any temptation to seek status in power rather than love. If we were more affectionately united with the tears of Jesus, we might be less anxious to exclude believers who do not agree with us in the details of doctrine and form.

The first evidence that we have been touched by Jesus' tears is an acknowledgment that *love* is the sign of a true disciple. Jesus says, "By this all men will know that you are my disciples, if you have love for one another" (John 13:35). If we fail to radiate the love of God in our lives, our achievements in doctrine and form will profit nothing. This is taught in Scripture with such force and clarity that only hardness of heart could miss it. "If I have prophetic powers, and understand all mysteries and all knowledge, and if I have all faith, so as to remove mountains, but have not love, I am nothing. If I give away all I have, and if I deliver my body to be burned, but have not love, I gain nothing" (I Cor. 13:2-3). Love crosses over denominational lines. It puts itself in another's place; it does as it would be done by.

When believers make a sincere effort to enter into each other's lives, they will not only give local expression to the unity for which Christ prayed, but they will be in a better position to extend this unity beyond themselves. They will appreciate why Christians in other traditions believe as they do. And when the warmth of these traditions is felt, believers will be less tempted to think that they enjoy exclusive access to grace and truth.

If the denominations are serious in their desire to liberate the fellowship from the confines of doctrine and form, they should take immediate steps to encourage interdenominational conversation. This can be done in many creative ways: by exchanging pulpits and seminary leadership, by arranging programs of personal visitation, and by the use of literature from other denominations. Every pastor should do his part to create a climate in which signs of fellowship are honored wherever they are found and under whatever conditions. And above all, status should be given to the prophet who stimulates a healthy discontent by reminding the church that form and doctrine are servants of the fellowship, and not the other way around.

Christians find their identity by personal confrontation with Christ. And the proof of this confrontation is not assent to doctrine, and certainly not membership in an institution. The proof is a gentle, outgoing charity that takes in all men, and especially those of the household of faith.

Surely it behooves the church to dedicate its energies to an adorning of the one virtue that makes man most like his Maker, and Christians most like their Lord.

If Christians would learn to love one another, the day might come when they would be willing to pray with one another, and perhaps even to confess their faults to one another. In that happy day the eyes of the understanding would be opened to see that the scandal of Christendom is not the plurality of denominations, but the manner in which believers seek status in doctrine and form, rather than love.

CHAPTER TWO

The Nature of the Unity We Seek

At the risk of being excessively negative, I shall try to show why orthodoxy finds it difficult to cooperate with the National and World Councils of Churches. The ethos of orthodoxy is seldom sympathetically understood. Critics tend to judge it by its worst, rather than by its best, elements.

Were I to name the criterion that inspires the best elements in orthodoxy, it would be the following: *The visible unity of Christendom is an ideal that simultaneously inspires and judges the real.* Just as we strive for sinless perfection, though we shall never reach it, so we strive for the equally valid, though equally elusive, ideal of visible unity. If a person imagines that the ideal can be realized in history, he betrays his own want of education. Either the terms of the ideal are underestimated or the possibilities of the real are overestimated. Since original sin tinctures the entire human enterprise, man's quest for unity is never a purely virtuous undertaking. Organizational security is partly a status symbol of pride and an outlet for will to power.

I am not saying that orthodoxy succeeds in applying its own principles. I only say that, in its finest moments, it evaluates the possibilities of Christian unity by what theologians call the "polar method." The ideal and the real must be kept in delicate balance.

I

While orthodoxy may err in its conviction—and I want to stress this possibility—it nevertheless believes that the ecumenical movement is plying a course that overlooks the effect of original sin on collective human efforts. And this oversight

Originally published in the Spring, 1957 issue of *Religion in Life*, traces back to a rather loose handling of the Word of God. Let me establish this by reviewing the kind of argument that appeals to the orthodox mind.

Christian unity is deceptively simple. Even a junior in seminary can define it. It is a fellowship of those who are spiritually joined with Christ in His life, death, and resurrection. "For by one Spirit we were all baptized into one body—Jew or Greeks, slaves or free—and all were made to drink of one Spirit" (I Cor. 12:13).[1] But if the definition of Christian unity is simple, its application is not. We unite when we sing the Te Deum, "We praise thee, O God," but we divide when we spell out the theology of this hymn. Our theology is never systematic, and unsystematic theology spawns disunity. This can be abundantly illustrated from the pages of church history, but I shall confine myself to two striking examples.

Luther and Zwingli tried to unite the Protestant cause, but "a different spirit" hindered them. Since they could not agree on the theology of Eucharist, division was unavoidable. And after centuries of theological debate, the Lutheran and Reformed efforts are no nearer union than on the eve of the Marburg Conference.

A similar difficulty frustrated the Reformed cause. Baptists contend that public profession of faith precedes the rite of baptism, while Presbyterians contend that covenant infants form an exception to this rule. Classical Baptist divines (John Gill, Abraham Booth, etc.) and classical Presbyterian divines (William Cunningham, B. B. Warfield, etc.) exhibit equal powers of critical acumen and personal piety. But apparently something more than this is required to exegete the fine points in the Bible. This is why the threat of division, like the poor, is with us always.

There is only one way to defeat this, and that is by making unity a higher virtue than truth. Romanism aptly illustrates the technique. Roman apologists cite our fragmented efforts as palpable proof that the Reformation principle defeats itself. But it should be observed that Roman apologists never tell us how the Vatican eliminates the threat of disunity. And there is good reason for this concealment, for if Roman strategy were really understood, the Catholic cause would fall into considerable disrepute.

The Vatican eliminates the threat of disunity by eliminating religious liberty. Unless a Roman Catholic surrenders his

[1] Scripture quotations are from the Revised Standard Version.

judgment to the Pope, he is excommunicated. But this species of unity holds no attraction to one who believes that man is made in the image of God and that freedom of inquiry is an indefeasible prerogative. Furthermore, Roman security is specious. A man must exercise religious liberty to evaluate a system that nullifies religious liberty. Before one can surrender his judgment to the Pope, and thus be safe, he must use his own fallible judgment to assure himself that the Pope is infallible. The complex criteria of verification must then be faced. Thus, if we trace Catholic confidence back far enough, it rests on the same peril of private judgment that led the Reformers to conclude that the Pope is not infallible. Where, then, is the Roman advantage? Orthodoxy fails to see any.

The Reformers had one goal in view, and that was to coax Roman theology into conformity with biblical truth. But Rome promptly answered by banishing the Reformers. This means that the genesis of our divisions traces back to the medieval church itself. Instead of meeting the Reformers on exegetical grounds, as Christ and the apostles met the Jews, Rome hurled barbed epithets of heresy and schism. The Reformers were given the curt option of either submitting to the tradition of the Church or of being excommunicated. To men of powerful Christian convictions, of course, this was not a live option at all. And Luther promptly showed his contempt by burning the papal bull.

II

Orthodoxy believes that the National and World Councils of Churches defend a position that is strikingly similar to that of Romanism. This is an audacious assertion, to be sure, but it rests on the solidest kind of evidence.

The Protestant principle received its first clarification in the Leipzig Disputation of 1519. When Luther said that the Council of Constance erred in condemning John Huss, it was plain to Eck, and Luther soon saw it, that two incompatible criteria were vying for primacy. Luther claimed the right of religious liberty, while Eck replied that this was one right Luther did not have. Since God has deposited the whole counsel of His will in the church diffusive, ecclesiastical tradition cannot be challenged by the opinion of an individual.

But Luther stood his ground. He knew that if a man surrenders his right to interpret Scripture according to the dictates of his conscience, whatever else remains is of very small account.

No wonder Carlyle called Luther's stand at Worms the greatest moment in the modern history of man. Luther thundered: "Unless I am persuaded by testimonies from Scripture or clear arguments,—for by themselves, I believe neither pope nor council—I stand convinced by the Holy Scriptures adduced by myself and my conscience is bound up in God's Word. Retract I do not and will not, for to do anything against conscience is unsafe and dangerous. Here I stand. I can do no otherwise. God help me. Amen."[2]

If the Reformation has done nothing else, it has clarified what is perhaps the most important theological question in this or in any other age. *Do we find the truth by submitting to the church, or do we find the church by submitting to the truth?* Rome defends the first possibility, while the Reformers defend the second. But a choice *must* be made; the option is forced. Rome contends that the truth is where the church is, while the Reformers contend that the church is where the truth is.

If Rome is right, we have only one course before us, and that is to recant our Reformation heritage and return with haste to the papal fold. We cannot plead indefectible ignorance. Moreover, Romanism boasts a consummate order of visible unity. To create a Protestant counterpart would be a very foolish expedient.

But if Rome is wrong, then it seems to orthodoxy that Protestants ought to have the moral courage and the intellectual honesty to live by their own principles. The moment we defend man's right to bind his conscience by a free and open study of Scripture, we are on Reformation soil and divisions in the church are both natural and necessary.

To say this, however, does not mean that divisions are either desirable or good. Such an outcome would offend the biblical ideal. To speak of *spiritual* unity without *visible* unity, what is this but to utter a contradiction? If a family will not live together, it is not a family at all. I now mean to say, even as I shall continue to mean to say, that divisions in the church *are* evil. As long as a single believer is outside the fellowship, love is incomplete.

To develop the problem more fully, let us return to Martin Luther and the problem of tragic moral choices. A choice is tragic, and thus invites admiration, when circumstances force one to decide between levels of good. Tragic moral choices

[2] Translation by David S. Schaff.

are always difficult to make, for they entail a compromise between the ideal and the real. Protestants should remember that the great schism in Western Christianity was the direct fruit of a tragic moral choice. Otherwise they will overestimate the possibilities of human virtue.

Martin Luther did not want to disturb the visible unity of Christendom. But he did not see how such a disturbance could be avoided, for the gospel of Rome and the gospel of Scripture were different gospels. A tragic moral choice had to be made. Luther had to decide between a united church that taught error and a divided church that at least allowed for the possibility of truth. And being bound by the Word of God, he threw himself on the higher alternative. *When a decision must be made between unity and truth, unity must yield to truth; for it is better to be divided by truth than to be united by error.* We test the church by truth, not truth by the church. The apostles judged the Christian community by the norm of divine revelation.

Each generation must make this same tragic moral choice—and not only once, but again and again. If we want the comfort of the Christian gospel, we must accept the distress of a divided church. When men are free to unite in Christ, they are also free to divide in Christ. Religious liberty brings dissension, and dissension brings disunity. "For there must be factions among you in order that those who are genuine among you may be recognized" (I Cor. 11:19). If we remove the threat of factions, we corrupt the very matrix of evangelical confrontation.

Sincere and unavoidable divisions should excite a sense of honor, not shame, in us. Milton wisely observes, "It is written that the Coat of our Saviour was without seam: whence some would infer that there should be no division in the Church of Christ. It should be so indeed; Yet seams in the same cloath, neither hurt the garment, nor misbecome it; and not only seams, but Schisms will be while men are fallible."[3] An unfettered gospel is the important thing.

Whenever orthodoxy ponders the goals of the ecumenical movement, it feels that the issue of the Reformation must be raised all over again. Rome says that truth is decided by the church. And judging by the rising tide of Protestant ecclesiasticism, the Roman position is attracting a legion of new converts. The ecumenical movement sees the evil in disunity,

[3] *Of True Religion, Heresie, Schism and Toleration,* in *Works of John Milton,* Columbia University Press, VI, 176-177.

and for this it must be praised. But it does not see the evil in untruth, and for this it must be criticized. Whether in Rome, Amsterdam, or Moscow, it makes no difference; truth *still* ranks above unity.

There is only one live heresy in the eyes of the National and World Councils of Churches, and that is the heresy of not cooperating with the National and World Councils of Churches. If a person cooperates, his defection from the Word of God is relegated to a place of tertiary importance. But this is precisely the theological climate that forced the Reformation. Luther was a heretic because he dared to say that the church is where truth is, and not the other way around. Orthodoxy is proud to take its stand with Luther.

III

To make its position as attractive as possible, the ecumenical movement has reduced Christian commitment to what it believes is a decisive creedal minimum. The 1948 Amsterdam assertion says, "The Ecumenical Council is a union of Churches which accept our Lord Jesus Christ as God and Savior." This is a praiseworthy confession, but it is not praiseworthy enough to suit orthodoxy, for the only heresy it catches is unitarianism. The holes in the mesh are so wide that a sea of theological error can swim safely through. This proves that the ecumenical movement is more concerned with unity than it is with truth.

Furthermore, the Amsterdam assertion is in direct conflict with Scripture. "Not every one who says to me, 'Lord, Lord,' shall enter the kingdom of heaven, but he who does the will of my Father who is in heaven" (Matt. 7:21). This verse asserts that unless a confession of Christ's lordship is united with an evangelical affection to do the will of God, it profits nothing. And where is the will of God, if not in the system of holy Scripture?

The ecumenical movement ought to come to terms with the disturbing fact that at least one church exists which *accepts* our Lord Jesus Christ as God and Saviour, but which promptly anathematizes those who defend religious liberty as part of God's image in man. This is what makes ecumenical strategy so anomalous. How can the Amsterdam assertion compose the differences in Western Christianity, when it was not a cause of these differences in the first place? What the Reformers knew, but what the ecumenical movement does not seem to know, is that the schism in Western Christianity cannot be mended until Rome acknowledges man's right to bind his conscience by a free and open study of the Word of God. But this is a concession Rome will never make, for the very genius of her position rests on a negation of religious liberty.

The practices of the ecumenical movement baffle orthodoxy. For example, what can possibly be gained by extending olive branches of reconciliation to the papacy? These overtures are as embarrassing to Protestants as they are offensive to Catholics. Since Rome claims an absolute monopoly on grace and truth, it considers ecumenical overtures, however sincere, as nothing but loathsome evidences that the Protestant mutiny has not yet been crushed. Rome will not rest until it enjoys absolute ecclesiastical jurisdiction. It seems to me that the ecumenical movement ought to have the good sense to see this.

When Protestants want unity so badly that they are embarrassed by the Reformation, they may want it so badly that they will end up surrendering their judgment to the Pope. They will have their coveted unity, to be sure, but at the price of the Word of God.

Orthodoxy would like to entertain a more charitable attitude toward the ecumenical movement—and this irenic note should be taken in the best possible sense—but it is not sure how to go about the matter without violating Scripture. Since the meaning of Christianity was normatively defined by Christ and the apostles, the course before us is clear. We must conform our conscience to truth. If there is an extrabiblical way to know the mind of God, orthodoxy has never heard of it. The Bible, and only the Bible, tells us how an offended God will dispose of a sinful world.

When orthodoxy examines the Bible with an eye to truth, it confronts a series of doctrines that have equal authority to bind the conscience because they are delineated with equal power and lucidity — God as triune, God's image in man, the federal headship of the first Adam, the fall of man, the federal headship of the last Adam, and Christ's virgin birth, humanity and deity, sinless life, miraculous works, substitutionary atonement, bodily resurrection, ascension into heaven, and glorious return. There is nothing esoteric about these doctrines. They are all open and plain. They are all carried by the rights of language.

The Amsterdam assertion is included in the above doctrines. Orthodoxy rejoices over any testimony to the lordship of Christ. But because the ecumenical movement is content to select one doctrine out of a number that are delineated with equal power and lucidity, it betrays its indifference to the exegetical demands of the biblical system. And what is this but a return to the ethos of Romanism?

For example, Christ's resurrection is of such importance that not only is Christian fellowship inconceivable apart from the empty tomb, but the very coherence of the Christian world view turns on the empirical validity of this one event. "If Christ has not been raised, then our preaching is in vain and your faith is in vain" (I Cor. 15:14). Deny that Christ defeated death, and where is the good news?

This is very clear. But apparently it is not clear enough, for the ecumenical movement extends a cordial welcome to open antagonists of the resurrection. Whether Christ conquered death is apparently not important. The important thing is that we all get together under one roof. And the ecumenical movement does not take this stand because of any textual difficulties in the Bible, for First Corinthians is universally recognized as Pauline.

IV

If the visible unity of Christendom is ever realized, it will be a sad day for the gospel. Just as democratic freedom is preserved by a prudential balance of social interests, so the freedom of the gospel is preserved by a prudential balance of ecclesiastical interests. Orthodoxy is afraid that the ecumenical movement will upset this balance by taking too much power to itself.

And there is a good reason for this fear. The National Council of Churches not only pretends to speak for the whole of American Protestantism, but it thinks it is sufficiently virtuous to decide what religious activity is of God and what is not. O. Walter Wagner writes in the August 22, 1956 issue of *The Christian Century*, "Gone are the days when the airways were a wide-open range for the denominational demagogue who could afford to buy time, or for the fundamentalist fringe group that used them to sell its divisive wares. Today, prevailingly, public service time is granted to the radio and television commission of the local council of churches." This is most instructive strategy. The ecumenical movement takes away the prejudices of the demagogue and the anarchist, and in their place puts the prejudices of the ecumenical movement. It then caps its arrogance by calling this progress. The truth is that the right of religious liberty is being curtailed. When a single power controls religious broadcasting, what is this but ecclesiastical tyranny? In an effort to restore a reasonable balance of power, orthodoxy has had to create such counteragents as the National Religious Broadcasters and the Radio Commission.

Because sinners use power as an outlet of pride, no part of Christendom can speak for all of Christendom. Whenever bands of union become too tight, religious liberty is threatened. Voltaire may have been wide of the mark at many points, but he knew enough about human depravity to hit the mark when judging the relation between pride, power, and ecclesiastical pretense. "If one religion only were allowed in England, the government would very possibly become arbitrary; if there were but two, the people would cut one another's throats; but as there are such a multitude, they all live happy in peace."[4]

Orthodoxy believes that every prudent means should be used to heal the divisions in the Christian church. But before one Protestant denomination joins with another, it must examine its own distinctives in the light of the Word of God. If the exegetical ground of these distinctives is no longer conclusive, overtures of union may be undertaken. But if Scripture affords no such release, separation must remain. Under *no* conditions should truth be subordinated to unity. We are saved by faith in Jesus Christ, not by works of the law—and especially not by the law that the church should be visibly united. Our divisions will continue to scandalize the natural man, but this should not unhinge us. The message of the cross is also a scandal.

At an earlier point I admitted that orthodoxy does not succeed in applying its own principles. I want to reaffirm this as I close. If the ecumenical movement tends to upset the biblical balance from one side, orthodoxy tends to upset it from the other. The ecumenical movement sees the perils in a divided, but not in a united, church; while orthodoxy sees the perils in a united, but not in a divided, church. The one error leads to tyranny, the other to anarchy. And the anarchy is no less reprehensible than the tyranny. Orthodoxy overlooks the work of sin in the separatist himself. Since the separatist does not belong to the National and World Councils of Churches, he thinks he is virtuous. This is a pathetic illusion, however, for status by negation is a far

[4] *Letters on the English*, Letter VI, "On the Presbyterians."

cry from affirmative righteousness. Orthodox doctrine, unsavored by orthodox love, profits nothing.

I am sorry about one thing. I am sorry that orthodoxy hesitates to take an active part in the modern dialogue about unity. I should think that the possession of truth would issue in a passionate desire to guide, rather than chide, the groping efforts of a tragically divided church. Failing in this nobler role, orthodoxy has merited its disrespect.

What shall we say, then, is the nature of the unity that we seek? *It is a fellowship in Jesus Christ that is vitally united with the system of biblical truth.* Fellowship is the flesh, while truth is the bones. Flesh without bones is flabby, while bones without flesh are dead. Together they make for organic unity.

CHAPTER THREE

Conservatives and Liberals Do Not Need Each Other

The title of this article seems to suggest an approach that is both heartless and offensive, if not sub-Christian. *But I am speaking solely and exclusively about the fact that conservatives and liberals in no way draw essential nourishment from each other when attempting to develop a systematic relation between human existence and ultimate reality.* This deliberately restricted frame of reference *must* be understood and appreciated; otherwise I shall give the impression of being a plain fool. I want to make as plain as the English language can put it that I would be among the first to contend that conservatives and liberals must work hand in hand whenever means can be devised to improve the general good of mankind. We might think, for example, of the promotion of social justice, the stabilization of political and economic forces in the nation, the improvement of public education, the cultivation of friendly ties between neighbors, and the offer of help to victims of a disaster.

Certainly it is a cause for no small sorrow that Protestantism is divided into such ideologically competitive camps as conservatives and liberals. What joy would result, if all who professed to be followers of Jesus Christ were to arrive at the unity of the faith.

Existing divisions in theology do not excuse acts of personal hatred, for the responsibility to love all human beings is repeatedly set forth with such solemnity in Scripture that an unloving Christian is a manifest contradiction in terms. Christians are confronted with a universal duty to love at the very moment they surrender their lives to Him who died a sacrificial death on the cross. Consequently, the law

Originally published in the May 21, 1965 issue of *Christianity Today*. Reprinted by permission.

of love may not be taken lightly, as if we have the privilege of deciding whether to be loving or unloving, depending upon how a particular person happens to affect us. Christians are commanded to love all men, everywhere. And if we ever have occasion to doubt this, we need only remind ourselves that Jesus Christ defended the law that we must love even our enemies.

Taking their eyes off their own inconsistencies, however, liberals now and then seem to derive a measure of consolation from the charge that conservatives are not true to the ideal of Christian love. This can be illustrated by the energy expended to see that the Reformers themselves are openly criticized. The crux of this criticism, whether valid or not, is that the Reformers labored so hard to develop a systematic interpretation of Scripture that they not only credited their interpretation with a finality it did not deserve but went on to vilify those who understood Scripture in a somewhat different way.

Actually, the only charge against the Reformers that is relevant is that they tended to be somewhat inconsistent when they went about the task of translating their philosophical and theological presuppositions into useful daily guides. After rigorously defending the divine quality of Scripture, they occasionally entertained the fallacy that love for a dissenter carried with it approval of the dissenter's error. Fallacies of this sort continue to tincture the testimony of the conservative.

Still, this in no way places the conservative in need of the liberal. It is a plain and observable fact that consistent, contemporary conservatives readily admit that they have no more than a partial grasp of God's whole counsel as revealed in Scripture. Moreover, this admission tends to make them more charitable toward those who, after no small dedication of mind and spirit, view the system of Scripture in a somewhat different light. Not all conservatives are charitable, of course, but neither are all liberals. Whenever the right conditions for it prevail, hatred rears its ugly head in every race under the sun: red, yellow, black, or white.

It should be pointed out, however, that the limited perspective that accompanies finitude is at best only a secondary reason why love toward all human beings is a basic imperative. The primary reason is the ethical teaching of the Christian system itself; and the conservative finds no justifiable ground for turning from this system. Jesus Christ loved God and neighbor with the whole of His person, and it is the sacred responsibility of all who profess the name of Jesus Christ to do likewise. Moreover, the Apostle Paul set forth a definitive list of love's attributes in the thirteenth chapter of First Corinthians. His language is so lucid that there is no need for supplementary standards. Some parts of Paul's epistles are difficult to understand, of course. Even the Apostle Peter acknowledged this. But it is quite enough if both the nature and the necessity of love are revealed through language that is easily understood.

True love for a person implies an act of unconditional acceptance. All human beings are made in the image of God, and the solemnity of this fact is in no way invalidated by the tendency of some people to think evil thoughts and perform evil deeds. Even those who put our Lord to death on the cross were made in the image of God, and Jesus Christ set a perfect example for all Christians when He manifested love for His slayers.

Unless this biblically revealed distinction between a person and his conduct is seriously accepted, misguided zealots—conservative or liberal—may end up clothing themselves with the garments of a new pharisaism. In other words, they will presume that they are righteous because they are not like others. This is no innocent error. Its substance may justly be called status by negation; and negative status, the most highly developed claim of a Pharisee, owes nothing to the redemptive work of Jesus Christ. If personal righteousness can be acquired by the trivial fact of not being like others, any reference to the gospel, however pious and eloquent, is little more than idle talk.

With this description of the ethical primacy of love before us, let us now turn to a brief discussion of the rational primacy of truth. This will help us put a cap on the topic under consideration.

As a convenient transition, let us reflect on an ideological error that some naive conservatives commit in handling Christian truth. They bow their heads and solemnly assert that the quality of religious infallibility is confined to Scripture, only to turn right around and piously presume that their particular interpretation of Scripture is also infallible. Such an error seriously disturbs the liberal mind, and rightly so. As a direct fruit of this error, these conservatives complacently imagine that they enjoy a monopoly on Christian truth, and that nothing whatever would be gained by entering into exploratory conversations with others who are also sincerely attempting to understand the meaning of Scripture as the revealed Word of God.

Since this kind of error traces to inconsistency, however, it is a warning that conservatives should be more faithful to their own presuppositions, and not a sign that conservatives need liberals.

This leads to another matter. Since conservatives are dedicated to the conviction that the Bible contains a divinely revealed system of truth, they tend to become so absorbed with yesterday's world that they pay little attention to issues peculiar to the world of today—so the liberal charges, anyway. Or to put it another way, the changing features of life are seemingly thought irrelevant. The present is neglected because the past is absolutized, and this supposedly spells the end of Christianity.

From all of this, it would seem to follow that conservatives need liberals, for liberals presumably will not rest until they have made a conscientious effort to see that the claims of the Christian faith are stated in such a way that they are relevant to the peculiar needs of modern man.

But this inference carries no force, because it is meaningless to speak about the claims of the Christian faith unless we are first of all persuaded that these claims are objectively true. This is why the conservative dogmatically insists that love and truth must be simultaneously respected. Christian truth accounts for the Church's time-tested conviction that God inspired holy men to declare the plan of salvation on divine authority. This conviction not only embodies the precise, systematic teaching of Scripture itself but also gratifies a basic need that the soul senses the moment it entertains judgments about the nature of God and God's revelation to the human race. Unless our religious convictions grow out of a divinely revealed system of truth, we shall have no means by which to be certain that *anything* is holy, not even love itself. This is probably the crucial reason why a conservative refuses to surrender his conviction that Scripture contains the only infallible rule of faith and practice. If God fails to disclose the manner in which He plans to deal with His creation, human beings have no more of a rational basis for faith and hope than does a tree.

In other words, nothing possesses ultimate authority and importance unless it can be validated by divinely revealed truth. The reason for this ought to be rather obvious. Suppose we have great wealth and enjoy perfect health; suppose we exercise awesome talents and wield immense powers; still, unless we are able to rest in a divinely validated answer to the question, "What must I do to be saved?" everything about us is hollow or empty.

Thus it is fallacious to say that conservatives and liberals need each other, for liberals simply do not believe that a divinely validated plan of salvation has been entrusted to the church. Liberals are so dedicated to the vision of making the Christian religion relevant to the supposed needs of modern man that they consider it a handicap to be checked by the rights of language in Scripture. Conservatives may now and then overlook new means and methods by which to confront modern man, and for this oversight they deserve criticism. But the fact remains, despite this just ground for criticism, that conservatives are sincerely trying to make peace with the revealed will of God.

Liberals doubtless mean well, but they invariably nullify the divinity of the gospel by the manner in which they subordinate the data of Scripture to data drawn from contemporary science and philosophy. This may strike some readers as a rather prejudiced and heartless judgment, but actually it is nothing more than a plain statement of fact. It is true that liberals sometimes claim to experience an encounter with God through the reading of Scripture, but this should never be confused with a whole-soul submission to the rights of language in Scripture.

If the church has been entrusted with a plan of salvation that is true on divine authority, then the relevance of Christianity is automatically established by the fact that it is true. To try to impose any other standard of relevance is manifestly wrong. What God says is final; even the slightest mishandling of Scripture is altogether out of order.

Liberals heavily emphasize love, and they often translate their convictions into praiseworthy acts of love. But they are less concerned to show how the highest act of love correlates with the highest statement of truth. If it is true that Jesus Christ died on the cross to save sinners, have we any right to say that we love sinners if we fail to confront them with this truth? And where can we find a divinely validated account of this truth apart from Scripture? In sum, we can express no higher love to lost humanity than to preach the gospel in the precise form in which God has been pleased to reveal it.

The intimate tie between love and truth can easily be illustrated. Let us suppose that some miners are sealed underground because of a huge landslide. Although communication with the trapped men is established, it seems inevitable that they will die of suffocation. But suppose an engineer in town is aware of a cave through which the trapped miners can crawl to escape their apparent doom. Unless the engineer shares this information clearly and accurately, he has no right to say that he loves the helpless miners.

No doubt someone will challenge our concept of highest love by citing John 15:13, "Greater love has no man than this, that a man lay down his life for his friends." The challenge can be met if we agree that Jesus is speaking of the greatest expression of love between *friends*. Certainly the last and highest proof of love for a friend is the act of substitutionary death. But a state of true friendship does not exist between a Christian and lost sinners when a Christian deliberately withholds the good news of the gospel. This follows from the fact that personal reconciliation with God is more important than earthly security. Earthly security is temporal, while reconciliation with God is eternal.

It might seem that liberals, in their zeal to make Christianity relevant to modern man, would derive some sort of stabilizing element from the conservative position. It is rather well known that liberalism tends to identify Christianity with the latest viewpoint, a procedure doomed to continue forever. But in fairness to the liberal position, it should be pointed out that dedicated liberals consider changing conditions of truth as worthy of praise, not scorn. Change, according to liberal standards, is a healthy sign that the human race is making progress. This is why the liberal becomes suspicious whenever he is confronted with the claim that material truth can be developed to the point where it is the same for all generations.

Hence the inference simply cannot be avoided that conservatives and liberals do not need each other. Since liberals look with disdain on fixed material truth, they also look with disdain on conservative presuppositions. When something is *not* needed, it is altogether futile to argue that it *is* needed. This is such a crucial part of the thesis under discussion that it merits restatement in another paragraph.

A consistent conservative, as we have pointed out above, believes that Scripture contains an account of a plan of salvation that is true on divine authority. Now, unless a liberal forthrightly and emphatically repudiates this particular view of Scripture, there simply would *be* no such person as a liberal in the first place. Therefore, since the very uniqueness of liberalism comes into existence with the repudiation of all claims to fixed and final truth as indispensable elements in the Christian faith, how can it be claimed that liberals need conservatives?

The only thing liberals really need is the steady flow of evidences that comes from daily thought and experience. Certainly conservatives do not believe that such evidences are sufficient to answer man's questions about the nature of God and of God's will for the human race. But the convictions of conservatives, when treated by liberal standards, bear no essential relation to the particular issues that concern modern man; and thus they may be dismissed as irrelevant.

When all is said and done, therefore, it is just about as meaningful to say that palm trees and icebergs need each other as it is to say that conservatives and liberals need each other. Certainly some element of mutual need exists, but the need is not essential.

CHAPTER FOUR

Orthodoxy: Cultic vs. Classical

Part One

I finished graduate studies in 1949. Being irenic in disposition, I wanted to go about the work of the gospel in a quiet, unassuming way. My goal was to defend a sane Protestant orthodoxy that was willing to be corrected on secondary issues because it was clear on primary issues. I never reached my goal.

The trouble began with—of all things—my use of the Revised Standard Version of the Bible. I was not charged with indiscretion, but with outright heresy, by a number of orthodox churchmen. At first I decided to ride out the storm, making no defense before my accusers. But in due season I sensed that a principle was at stake. Is *Christ* the Lord of the conscience, or is orthodoxy? Once the question assumed this form, I knew I would have to play the polemicist, whether I wanted to or not. As Luther realized in his own day, the time to speak had come, the time to be silent had passed.

Why was orthodoxy so hostile toward the Revised Standard Version? This was the question that disturbed me, for I had always assumed that Protestants rejoiced when the Word of God was translated into the vernacular. I could easily forgive the laymen who attacked me, for they acted on higher orders. But what about the clergymen who plotted this war of nerves? Though they lacked a scholar's command of Hebrew and Greek, they were not shy to storm the divinity schools of the land, there to rail against the retiring members of a translation committee. The very thought of this unholy crusade filled my heart with sorrow.

I realized that the Revised Standard Version has its share of faults. The conjectural emendations in the Old Testament, for example, leave much to be desired. Still, the RSV sets forth the gospel in plain, forthright language, and in this I rejoiced. I think it is a mistake to entomb the Word of God within the seventeenth-century language forms of the King James Version. If we *must* choose between beauty and clarity, for the sake of the common man let us choose clarity.

Orthodoxy was particularly impatient with the RSV translation of Isaiah 7:14. The rendition "young woman" (I think "maiden" would have been better) was taken as a theological attack on the virgin birth of Christ. This reaction was unfortunate, for it betrayed a serious deficiency in biblical hermeneutics. The Old Testament is to be interpreted by the New Testament, not the other way around.

After due reflection I concluded that orthodoxy suffered from a serious illness. The symptoms were too clear to be missed. Orthodoxy has at times denied modernists the most elementary civil courtesies; it has subtly evaded Christian social action and cooperative church ventures. But I could not accuse orthodoxy without accusing myself, for I was a direct offspring of orthodoxy. I soon found that my own heart was hardened. I forgot that Jesus names *love,* not possession of doctrine, as the sign of a true disciple. I corrupted the communion of the saints by refusing to hold friendly, exploratory conversation with Christians of other traditions; I was more anxious to correct than to be corrected. This was a painful admission, but it served as a spiritual catharsis. It prepared me for the delicate task of judging my own heritage. I knew what was wrong with orthodoxy because I knew what was wrong with myself.

During graduate studies I presumed that American orthodoxy was a pure, unified witness to the system of truth in Scripture. A little experience on the field showed that I erred. American orthodoxy is a house divided against itself. Two schools of thought vie for leadership.

The first school is cultic orthodoxy. The cult lives by mores and symbols of its own devising; it makes no effort to join fellowship with the church universal. The more belligerent elements in orthodoxy come from this school.

The second school is classical orthodoxy. The followers of

this position are impatient with the small talk of the cult; they long for authentic conversation on historic themes. Most younger men, especially those who have taken time to get a decent education, belong to this school.

Cultic orthodoxy draws its followers from two main sources. First, it attracts those who are separatists by nature. These people enjoy greater liberty, or reap greater glory, by going it alone. They have little concern for the fortunes of the church universal. They found independent churches, independent schools and independent mission boards. Second, cultic orthodoxy attracts those whose theological attitudes have been warped by the fundamentalist-modernist controversy. These people turn to the cult as a refuge from the presumed apostasy of the historic denominations. They defend the church universal in their theology, but they do little to translate this defense into an outreaching program of fellowship.

For the sake of semantic clarity, I have decided to designate cultic orthodoxy by the term "fundamentalism." Although the fundamentalist movement dissolved many years ago, the mentality of fundamentalism has remained a fixed feature of the cult.

I reserve the term "orthodoxy" for classical orthodoxy. I know of no enlightened conservative who wants to perpetuate the ethos of fundamentalism. The struggle between fundamentalism and modernism may have been unavoidable, but this is no reason why elements in the modern church should be locked in prejudice. And that goes for everyone professing the name of Christ. A lot has happened in the past twenty-five years. With the decay of the Wellhausen hypothesis and the return to biblical theology, the time is ripe for mutual signs of humility. The issues are not nearly as neat as either fundamentalism or modernism imagined.

The doctrine of the church is the dividing line between fundamentalism and orthodoxy, and the line is a sharp one. Fundamentalism rests its case on a separatist view of the church. It contends that when a denomination has modernists among its clergy or missionaries, a Christian must withdraw financial support until said modernists are deposed. And if financial boycott fails, a Christian must disaffiliate forthwith; he must start a "pure witness" for the gospel.

When I first began to preach the Word of God, I paid little attention to the difference between fundamentalism and orthodoxy. But after a few encounters with fundamentalism I realized I was not a separatist by nature, nor could I discover any biblical warrant for the separatist position. To the contrary, all relevant evidence pointed in the other direction. Let me cite samples of this evidence.

The believing community in the Old Testament was often blemished by ungodly kings and false prophets. But the true prophets of God did not separate themselves on that account, nor were the laity any less obliged to bring their tithes and offerings into the storehouse.

Jesus remained in communion with the temple, though scribes and Pharisees taught there, though Annas and Caiaphas ministered at its altars, and though corruption was so widespread that the office of high-priesthood was put up for the highest bidder. Jesus worshiped in the temple and taught in the synagogues because the oracles and ordinances of God were there. He denounced separatism by His express example.

The Book of Revelation clearly points out the defects of seven churches. But these defects supplied neither cause nor occasion for schism. Separation from these churches would have implied separation from Jesus Christ and John His apostle. The seven churches had the true canon of Scripture and the true sacraments, dispensed by apostolic ministry.

From this and other evidence I concluded that fundamentalism had formulated its view of the church with an eye to the interests of the cult. Fundamentalists believe they are superior because they have withdrawn from the historic denominations; they imagine that they alone glorify the gospel. Since the fundamentalist is deprived of the happy security that comes from communion with the church universal, he must devise substitute securities all his own. And the handiest substitute—the one calling for the least energy and skill—is to appear better by making others appear worse. In plain language, the fundamentalist tattles, because censure implies superiority.

This explains why fundamentalism took such an intolerant attitude toward the Revised Standard Version. Ever occupied with the work of negative status, the fundamentalist must blame others for evil; he must find a scapegoat. So, the modernists on the translating committee were considered fair game. And when I preached from the RSV, I was charged with giving aid and comfort to modernism.

Since orthodoxy is willing to hold friendly, exploratory conversation with Christians of other traditions, I think that orthodoxy should be invited to the tables of theological discussion. When liberalism dismisses orthodoxy as a refuge of ignorance, it manifests the same signs of cultic thinking that protrude so conspicuously in fundamentalism.

If we are going to bear true witness to the body of Christ we must temper our zeal with kindness, for love is the sign of a true disciple. Love does not rejoice in evil; it puts itself in the place of another; it does as it would be done by.

Let me say why I think that orthodoxy should be invited to the tables of theological discussion. Theologians now know, if they have never known it before, that man has a moral defect in his will and in his affections. This defect has been revealed in the brutality of two world wars; it has been corroborated by the clinical findings of depth psychology. In an effort to grapple with the reality of human sin, theologians have wisely reaffirmed the doctrine of justification by faith. Unless God accepts us by the righteousness of Christ we are undone, for in ourselves we cannot defeat pride and pretense. But the moment we rest in positional righteousness we must deal with the problem of religious authority. The logic of justification could not be discovered by human wisdom, nor is it imparted by personal confrontation with Jesus Christ. It is discovered by a patient, exegetical submission to Scripture—to Romans and Galatians, in particular, for they are the places where justification is treated in systematic, didactic form. When we take the work of exegesis seriously, we face issues that orthodoxy has faced for quite a long time. Not to draw on the experience of orthodoxy would, I feel, be new evidence of cultic pride.

In defending the normative character of Romans and Galatians I am not trying to brew unrest in the church, nor am I turning my back on the legitimate claims of biblical criticism. Rather, I am addressing myself to an issue that decides the very foundations of Protestant hermeneutics. Only as we anchor hope in objective evidence will we be delivered from the sorry business of gaining status by negating each other. Even our mistakes, when made in the name of Christ, are covered by justification. We need not try to seem better by making others seem worse, for Christ is our righteousness. He paid the full debt of sin.

When I say that believers of various traditions should come to know each other, I do not say that we should organize some sort of super-church. Under these conditions original sin would only express itself in new forms of ecclesiastical tyranny. But I do say that we should not rest until we have created a genuine unity in the Holy Spirit. And the first evidence of this unity is a spiritual willingness to respect one another's convictions. We do not understand the nature of the church because we do not understand one another. We *are* the church, whether we acknowledge the relation or not. We belong to one another, with Christ as our head.

The fundamentalist continues to go it alone because he fears that friendly conversation will lead to theological compromise. His fear traces to an imperfect grasp of the Word of God. When we communicate with the church, we do not communicate with the errors of individual members. We communicate only in the truth, the truth bequeathed by Christ and the apostles.

Perhaps the day will come when the fundamentalist will temper his separatism by the wisdom of the ages. Perhaps not. But in the meantime let us not be too disturbed by his vanity. The fundamentalist means well. He wants status in the church, but he errs in the way he goes about getting it. Having missed the way, he needs our pity, not our scorn.

Part Two

Let me say a word about that anxious breed of younger men who are conservative in theology but are less than happy when they are called "fundamentalists." These men are both the cause and the effect of a radical atmospheric change within American orthodoxy.

The fundamentalist movement was organized shortly after the turn of the present century. It served as a rallying point for a host of gifted and not-so-gifted conservatives, who rushed to do battle with modernism. The charge was that modernism had surrendered the gospel to German higher criticism and to extravagant social philosophies patterned after biological evolution. Subsequent events, such as the disintegration of modernism and the return to biblical theology, show that the fundamentalist movement was not tilting against windfalls.

But if such is the case, why did the movement fall into general disrepute? The answer is quite within reach. Through a series of subtle internal changes, fundamentalism shifted

Part Two of this chapter was first published under the title, "Post-Fundamentalist Faith," copyright© 1959, Christian Century Foundation. Reprinted by permission from the August 26, 1959 issue of *The Christian Century*.

from an affirmation to a negation. The result was a cunning pharisaism that confused possession of truth with possession of virtue. Fundamentalism stood in the temple of God, thankful that it was not like modernism. Status by negation, not a humble reliance on the grace of God, served as the base for Christian security.

Having exempted itself from the scrutiny of divine righteousness, fundamentalism often took on the mannerisms of a pugnacious cult. The test of Christian discipleship was no longer "works done in love." The test was "assent to the fundamentals of the faith." In this way the foolishness of the cross was obscured by the foolishness of those who came in the name of the cross. Assent to doctrine is no match for demonic pretense, for even the devil can pass a course in Christian theology.

But fundamentalism made its crowning error when it enlisted the doctrine of the church in its quest for negative status. While the doctrine purported to come from Scripture, scrutiny showed that it derived from the conviction that possession of truth is the same thing as possession of virtue. And since only fundamentalists were in possession of truth, they alone were virtuous enough to form the body of Christ. All other elements in the Christian community were apostate.

It was by a discovery of this pompous theological error that I awoke from dogmatic slumber. I now realize, though once I did not, that the nature of the church is *never* measured by the doctrinal maturity of those who profess Christ. Doctrine clarifies the plan of salvation, but a sinner is justified by faith and repentance, not by assent to doctrine. Believers, in some cases, must overcome deeply embedded prejudices before they can appreciate either the scope or the relevance of Christian doctrine. But this deficiency, other things being equal, is no mark against the person. The want of doctrinal maturity, like the want of subjective holiness, is remedied by sanctification, not justification. When fundamentalism confined the body of Christ to those who received the system of revealed doctrine, it obscured the distinction between justification and sanctification. It returned, in effect, to the ethos of Roman Catholicism.

I know that much of this will sound elementary to outsiders. But to one reared in the tyrannical legalism of fundamentalism, the recovery of a genuine theology of grace is no insignificant feat. The feat calls for a generous outlay of intellectual honesty and personal integrity.

Since a goodly company of younger conservatives are trying to restore the classical lines of orthodoxy, philosophy of religion ought to reserve the term "fundamentalist" for the person who confuses possession of truth with possession of virtue or who defends a separatist view of the church. Unlike fundamentalism, orthodoxy does not affect a monopoly on truth. It rejects the cultic quest for negative status; it is ready to entertain friendly conversation with the church universal.

The term "orthodoxy," of course, is freighted with unfortunate connotations of its own. It often suggests either a sterile confessionalism or a provincial stand against progress. Still, it is a useful term, for it denotes the conservative tradition in Christian theology. I call myself orthodox because I cordially assent to the great doctrines of the faith. But I do not for one moment suppose that assent to doctrine is either the instrumental cause of justification or the touchstone of Christian fellowship. Were I to do so I would be reverting to fundamentalism.

It is too bad, in a way, that we have to use labels at all. In Antioch they were content to be called Christians. But all is not lost. By using carefully selected labels, we at least clarify our position in the theological spectrum. And once we are done with the business of semantics, we can turn to the really exciting item on the agenda of faith: sharing fellowship with all who love Jesus Christ and who are willing to test and correct their partial insights by the full insight of God's Word.

CHAPTER FIVE

On Faith and Reason

There can be no question but that Søren Kierkegaard gave a profoundly convincing defense of the third locus of truth.* What Christianity has always assumed, Kierkegaard made explicit. . . .Saving faith is not simply an intellectual assent to objective facts. Faith is cordial trust; it is a concerned, inward response to the person and work of Jesus Christ. Until the end of time, therefore, men who remember what it means to be a person will defend the supremacy of truth as inwardness. God sent His Son to make us *good,* not simply to make it possible for us to recite the creeds of the church.

But what must be questioned is the prudence of Kierkegaard's attempt to secure inward truth by opposing it to objective evidences. It is from *his* lips, not those of the biblical writers, one learns that faith must believe what the understanding finds contradictory — and for that very reason. Scripture's healthy balance of the loci of truth has been upset by Kierkegaard. Rationality was bequeathed by Jesus Christ as a light by which men may penetrate the darkness of error. "The true light that enlightens [gives a spiritually rational nature to] every man was coming into the world" (John 1:9). Being a rational creature, thus, man must proportion his

* In his later writings, Carnell devoted much time and space to what he called "the third locus of truth" (truth in the heart) or "the third way of knowing." (See Chapter Six in this volume.) This was a departure from what he regarded as an excessive rationalism in his first book, *An Introduction to Christian Apologetics.* It was also a concession to what he viewed as a moment of truth in such Christian existentialists as Søren Kierkegaard. However, Carnell continued throughout his life to deplore the tendency of many Christian thinkers (e.g., Kierkegaard, Barth, etc.) to divorce faith from reason. This chapter, taken from Carnell's *Philosophy of the Christian Religion* (Grand Rapids, Eerdmans, 1952), begins with a critique of Kierkegaard and then applies this same line of reasoning to contemporary neo-orthodoxy.

spiritual commitments to what the mind can conscientiously clear. Apart from this distribution of authority edification is impossible.... Saving faith germinates only after the mind is first convinced of the sufficiency of the evidences. If Christ taught plain logical nonsense... a balanced man would turn aside from Him as one to be pitied, not trusted. The reason why we are able to trust Christ is that He spoke and lived in a way which is congenial with our axiological expectations.

Faith and Reason in Daily Life

There is nothing offensive about the Scriptural insistence that faith be based on a co-operative activity of spirit and mind, for it is the very arrangement we are obliged to respect in all conscious activity. We commit ourselves in faith to—that is, we act with concern over—only what is reasonable. The faculty of intelligence is the guide of our lives. By its word we conclude that since the alarm has rung it is time to arise; that this hallway leads to the bathroom; that this is our toothbrush in front of us; that these are our children with us at breakfast; that the driveway is clear as we back our automobile out; that the signals in traffic mean what they say; that the building ahead contains the office in which we must labor for the day, etc. *And in no case do we act passionately in defiance of the report of reason.* The only way a person can maintain both social respect and personal sanity is to proportion his commitment to the veraciousness of the evidences which the understanding processes. When reason assures us that our automobile is the blue one parked just beyond yonder sign, we dare not passionately believe against the understanding that the brown car over to the left belongs to us. Suppose that a person, having generated enough passion to act in opposition to the understanding, concluded: "My understanding tells me that this is a porcupine, but I passionately believe that it is my loving wife." If he existentially acts upon this urge, the results will be interesting. The porcupine will be perplexed, the wife greatly resentful, and the individual filled with quills. In any case the terminal value could hardly commend itself to a person who remembers he is made in the image of God.

If our conduct in life is able to suggest any axiom, it is the following: *The native person—the one unaffected by corrupting philosophic presuppositions—is at his best, and is most ideally a man of faith, when he obeys, rather than defies, the report of a critically developed understanding.* If my understanding assures me that I cannot drive through the darkness ahead because a bridge has been washed out, I come to grief when I permit my inward passion for crossing to go in defiance of the evidences. Faith may *remove* mountains, but it cannot declare mountains to be non-mountains.

The Controversial Exception

At this point, Kierkegaard [might interrupt] to say that the above discussion is entirely beside the point. Not only does he grant that *nous* is part of the *imago dei*—and thus is the daily guide in our practical affairs—but that all praise belongs to the understanding for the regal authority of its office. There is only one realm in which reason must be defied, and that is when our eternal happiness is at stake. Whenever time and eternity intersect, paradox results. It is at this point that objectivity brings offense to the understanding. The finite cannot assimilate the infinite without facing paradox. To seek to construct a rational bridge between time and eternity is to assume the very attitude of sinful detachment and disdain which is characteristic of existential untruth. The very *desire* to meet God on congenial, rational terms is sinful. If the bride-to-be is offended to see her bridegroom calmly collect rational evidences to prove her existence, God is slashed in heart to have His own children leisurely move about the world, using strength supplied from Him, to accumulate evidences which make it rationally respectable for them to believe there is a God.

Kierkegaard appears firmly convinced that a faith which reposes in objectively veracious evidences is not a faith at all. Faith rises and falls in proportion to the risk the will must take in the leap of decision. One has no faith when doing mathematics, since all venture is missing; but infinite faith is generated when approaching God, for the proof of God's existence is the commitment itself. Any bridge to eternity apart from the existential witness is untruth . . . .

With all candor, however, one finds it impossible to concede Kierkegaard's thesis that in matters of eternal happiness we may—nay, *must*—go against the understanding. The obvious difficulty is that in our approach to eternal things . . . we doom our venture to defeat the instant we turn aside from a mindful respect of the degrees of objective evidence. If there is any realm where we should expect to rally all our faculties for one harmonious thrust toward truth, it is at the point where our eternal happiness is at stake. If the witness of daily life has another axiomatic insight to teach us, it is the following: *The obligation of the will to clear with the verdict of the understanding rises in direct ratio to the importance of the value at stake* . . . .

The principle illustrated here holds in every conceivable circumstance where the valuable is in the balance: The more a value increases, the more our concern should respect the report of reason. When a fleeing man comes to a fork in the road, knowing that one path leads to life while the other guides to death, he will critically examine the evidence and then act in harmony with the report of the understanding. Suppose he said, "My understanding tells me that if I go to the right I will find life; but in passionate faith I shall act against the understanding; for I will be complacent in my decision if I follow objective truth." One would label him unbalanced. *Worthy passion is aroused by the nature of the value in question, not the strength or weakness of the evidences which support it.*

And when the supreme value is brought into the discussion, namely, faith in God, the heart can think of absolutely no reason why the axiom which guides us in all other axiological situations should now suddenly fail. If God's existence is of infinite concern to us, we ought to express infinite determination to obey, rather than defy, the understanding . . . .

*Neo-orthodoxy and the Problem of Error**

[Religious modernism claimed], harking back to Schleiermacher, that *feeling* is the way to know God. If a man will only be sensitive to the still, small voice of God, he will feel the nearness of God and know the doctrine whether it be of God or man. To the modernist, the Bible is the history of man's experiences with God.

Now, if feeling is the test of religious truth, how can one draw the line between valid and invalid religious feeling? Some feel that there is one God; others feel that there are many gods. Some feel that Christ is the Son of God; others do not . . . . The obvious difficulty with Modernism's theory

*The material in this section is taken from Carnell's article, "The Problem of Religious Authority," which first appeared in the Feb., 1950 issue of *His*. Used by permission.

of knowledge [was] that it [could not] be tested for error. This is fatal for any epistemology. When a man cannot test a system for error, he cannot validate it, for he never knows but that his very claim to truth might be an instance of the error which his methods cannot test.

Neo-orthodoxy's much more subtle epistemology is far less easy to examine. This new method is explained by so much technological terminology that only the expert can understand it.

The following minimal presuppositions seem to emerge however:

What the modernist calls "feeling" neo-orthodoxy calls "crisis" (Karl Barth), "divine-human encounter" (Emil Brunner), or "dialectical tension" (Reinhold Niebuhr). Neo-orthodoxy then goes on to say that the Bible is authoritative as salvation-history (*Heilsgeschichte*), but not as ordinary history or science, and that it is in connection with the reading of this salvation-history that one enjoys the "crisis-encounter." The Bible is a stable reference, but it is not an objectively inspired document. Neo-orthodoxy goes along with destructive higher criticism in matters of historical or scientific fact which are unimportant to salvation-history, as does Modernism. For example, while the Bible affirms that there was both a historical Adam and a fall, neo-orthodoxy contends that each man is Adam and that the fall is the moment-by-moment experience of all men.

This is difficult epistemology. It needs more explanation. We would ordinarily think that to reveal Himself, God would do it in just about the same way we reveal our human selves to each other. When the act of revelation is over, those to whom it came have something which is completed, which can be studied and examined as a fact. Neo-orthodoxy, however, fearful lest revelation encourage dead orthodoxy, has defined the relation between time and eternity as a dialogue or a conversation, and says that a tensional relation between the two must be perpetual if revelation is to break through. Revelation is a conversation between a hidden God and a depraved sinner. Revelation is effective only when it shatters the individual by speaking to and against his pride. But because time and eternity are always incompatible, paradox results whenever they are brought together in the moment of revelation. The intellect is offended by what the heart finds to be true. The sinner is simultaneously condemned and justified. God is hidden and revealed at the same time.

The kingdom of God is not given, and yet it is here. The Bible is not, and is, God's Word. As an objective document lying hidden in the safe, it is just another claim to revelation; only when I speak with God in passionate interaction with salvation-history does the Bible become God's Word for me, they claim.

The crux of neo-orthodoxy is its attempt to separate salvation-history in the Bible from ordinary history, whereas the Bible claims to be divinely inspired on both counts. We look in vain for the slightest hint in the Scriptures themselves that the writers shifted in their claims to authority when they talked first about Adam and then about Christ, the second Adam. This is the heart of the problem: *If we cannot trust the Bible's account of itself, how can we trust its account of salvation-history?*

To be concrete: with the same breath the Bible's writers teach that there was a historical Adam and that this Adam is the prototype of Jesus Christ, the second Adam (Rom. 5:12ff.). Now, observe what the epistemology of the "divine-human encounter" does to this claim. Crisis theology affirms that it is the witness of the dialogue of the sinner with God that there was no Adam. This is a very serious epistemological claim, since it shows that the real thing in neo-orthodoxy is not an objective Bible but the subjective experience of the crisis encounter.

Neo-orthodoxy, in fact, turns out to be but an extension of the fallacy of modernism, for modernism has its own *Heilsgeschichte.* The feeling of God was normatively expressed in portions of the Bible. All that neo-orthodoxy has done is to increase this insight in the field of valid experience to include the salvation-history tension. But the intensification of a bad epistemology will not save it from the inherent weaknesses which attend it. Like modernism, neo-orthodoxy is a theology based on feeling.

For example, let us suppose that the crisis experience teaches me that Christ is *not* the Son of God and that the Bible has no salvation-history at all? Is not this encounter valid? Shall not this experience be just as acceptable on neo-orthodoxy's thermometer as the registration that there is no first Adam? The Apostle Paul was willing to let the validity of both Christ and the first Adam hang together. If one goes, the other goes likewise. Neo-orthodoxy believes that it has done a great epistemological service in dividing between history and salvation-history, but it fails to sense the implications of such a division. It would not take a Marxian long to have a crisis experience that cancels out the whole Christian framework as untrue. Should the Bible not fall in line with the kind of tension that his heart feels ought to be maintained between time and eternity, so much worse for the Bible, and so much the better for Communism.

The trouble with neo-orthodoxy is, once again, that it cannot test for error. It can no more recognize a valid crisis experience than the modernist can recognize a valid religious feeling.

Should the collective experience of the community be appealed to, even that would not settle the matter. Truth is not learned by counting noses. Furthermore, even if it be true that collective crisis experience has validated the second Adam to date, does it follow that Christ will be true tomorrow? Perhaps what was dialectically valid yesterday will be dialectically invalid tomorrow. We can only wait and see.

Nowhere does the Bible distinguish between ordinary and salvation-history. Jesus Christ affirmed both the historicity of Noah and the flood and the eschatological implications for salvation attending them. He showed absolutely no tone of difference in His authority when speaking of one or the other. Neo-orthodoxy, however, is trying to perform surgery on the text by teasing out the tissues of salvation-history from the cancer of ordinary history and science. But it does not realize that in so doing it has destroyed our basis for believing that the Bible is God's Word in any compelling sense. The doctrinal claim of the writers of the Bible is that they are telling the mind of God whenever they speak. And if this doctrine is wrong, why should their doctrine suddenly be right when they begin to speak about salvation-history?

A city newspaper would dismiss its reporters if they ever did what neo-orthodoxy charges that the writers of the Bible have done. Suppose that a large city fire were reported, only the name of the city was wrong; would that be a "slight matter of history" which the editor-in-chief would not worry about? Or suppose that the headlines read that a new president had been elected, except that on the historical matter of who this new president was, the paper erred; would that be just "a triviality"? Hardly. And yet we are asked by Brunner and Niebuhr to believe that, though the Bible blunders here and there about history, science, and psychology, it is God's valid salvation-history where the writers happen to speak things that coincide with our crisis experiences.

How can we trust Christ for the really important things of the soul if He is not even able to get simple historical matters straight.... When a man cannot put two and two together and get the right answer, he surely is not an advanced mathematician. If Christ blundered on data of simple history, how can He suddenly become an authority when He switches to salvation-history?

And if Christ deliberately accommodated Himself to tradition on historical matters, announcing them as truth when He knew they were not, then it is not easy to see how Christ has even the *moral* qualities to be our Saviour, let alone the knowledge. Generally, truth in the inward parts — even if the price be death — is a prime characteristic of a moral man.

The Apostle Paul was willing to throw Christianity away entirely if Christ was not bodily raised from the grave (I Cor. 15:14). Yet Niebuhr calls the resurrection a "myth," contending that salvation-history does not depend on the literal fact of the resurrection. What could be further from the truth? Can nothing stand for something and mean anything? If the resurrection never happened, it can no more be a symbol of our hope than can the fountain of youth, which never existed.

If faith and dogmatics have no part with philosophy and rational proof... the heart is bequeathed a bifurcation in knowledge which renders the conventional laws of philosophy impotent to test for the truth of revelation.* Then what test is there for a veracious crisis experience or divine-human encounter? Perhaps what we think is God overtaking us in Christ is either only an emotional disturbance or the by-product of a hidden disease. Since we use coherence to test for truth in all other realms, why should its power suddenly be ruled irrelevant where we need it most, namely, in the testing for revelation? These questions remain unanswered....

The Truth about Faith

It is extremely difficult to understand why it is necessary to antagonize faith's relation to rational evidences. Kierkegaard started off with a completely false prejudice in supposing that inwardness is jeopardized when the mind is satisfied with the consistency of objective evidences. It is *not* psychologically true that passionate concern increases in commensurate ratio

* This chapter now returns to Carnell's argument in the last chapter of his *Philosophy of the Christian Religion*.

to objective uncertainty. In our daily living, we *proportion* our inward response to the certainty of the evidences. Suppose, for instance, a man of questionable character comes to me and swears that my house is on fire; rather than being passionate over such objective uncertainty, I only shrug my shoulders and pass my way. Why become excited over nothing? If in the next minute I see smoke rising from the direction of my home, I now become somewhat concerned, though not greatly, for the smoke may be from a passing train. The evidences are not yet sufficient. But if a trusted friend rushes up and gasps out the words that my property is actually on fire, I then become aroused to great concern, for the evidences at last are fully trustworthy. I now passionately act upon the truth of what has been told me, my whole person being satisfied with its coherence. Thus, a faith based on rational evidences is able to nourish a healthy inwardness. But if faith were a passion grounded in objective uncertainty, then I should exhibit my best faith when I have no house, when there is no fire, and (alas) when I myself am not.

There is no convincing reason why time-eternity relations should stand outside of the conventional connections of rational coherence. If rationality does not form a univocal bond of meaning which significantly relates these two orders of being, not only is the venture of faith made difficult; it is rendered impossible. When God is not rationally related to us, we cannot trust Him for our salvation. Not only will we never understand what He says, on the one hand, but also we would never know whether He means to perform what He says, on the other.

There is no "leap" in faith. While faith may involve a cordial commitment of the whole man to Jesus Christ, it is a passion which is drawn out by objectively measurable evidences. Whenever spirit is satisfied that the evidences are sufficient, it rests in truth. One ought to repent, for example, only when he has been persuaded that it is an axiologically good thing so to do. Why repent if it is not worthwhile? Why believe in Christ if it is not a coherent act? Why be obedient to God's law if it is absurd? Truth is one, not many. Plato long ago realized that the world of Ideas is useful only if it is continuous with rationality as philosophers in the academies know it. The Christian stands in this tradition. Jesus Christ is worthy of our faith—and consequently ought to receive it—because both His person and His doctrine are rationally continuous with the values which we have already accepted in ordinary experience. We do not think dialectically when we do geometry, operate a battery of drill presses, drive our automobiles, or converse with friends. Why, then, should we suddenly do it when we either perform God's will, struggle within the tensions of morality, interpret the Scriptures, or converse with the Father in prayer? There is no cause for a shift. The same Lord of truth is sovereign in both heaven and earth; His mind gives meaning to both natural and special revelation.

CHAPTER SIX

Becoming Acquainted with the Person of God

When formulating a philosophy of life, I contend that the least accessible fact, and thus the most baffling to isolate and classify, is the complex moral and spiritual environment of the philosopher himself. Most efforts in abstraction fail to impress the common man because sages seldom take time to interpret life from within the center of their own perspective as individuals. The more carefully I have meditated on this, the more convinced I have become that a world view remains truncated to the degree that a thinker fails to deal with data gained by a humble participation in the moral and spiritual environment.

Philosophers err when they confine their attention to "universal man." There is only one real man: the suffering, fearing individual on the street; he who is here today and gone tomorrow; he whose heart is the scene of a relentless conflict between the self as it ought to be. Whenever a philosopher speaks of mankind in the abstract, rather than concrete individuals at home and in the market, he deceives both himself and all who have faith in his teaching.

What it means to be held in a moral and spiritual environment can only be learned as one acquaints himself with the realities that already hold him from existence itself. This pilgrimage into inwardness is a painfully personal responsibility, for only the individual himself has access to the secrets of his moral and spiritual life. The task cannot be wrought by proxy. It is sheer affectation to try to be another person. "We are not to judge of the feelings of others by what

Reprinted by permission from chapters one, two and six of Edward John Carnell's *Christian Commitment* (New York, Macmillan, 1957).

we might feel if in their place."[1] The particularities of selfhood are not open for public inspection; they lie too deep for discovery . . . .

Here, then, is the first clue to the third method of knowing: *Ultimate reality cannot be grasped unless rational knowledge is savored by spiritual conviction.* We do not know the significance of "dependence" until a mental awareness of this relation fructifies in a whole-souled adjustment to its claims. Dependence must be felt; it cannot be a mere object of thought. Even as guilt implies the feeling of culpability, and even as indebtedness implies the feeling of obligation, so dependence implies the feeling of subordination. Hence, a person does not rightly apprehend dependence until he conforms himself to the relation. The necessity of this conformity is included in the relation itself. If an individual *professes* to be dependent, while he lives as if he were self-sufficient, he deceives himself and the truth is not in him. His proud life shows that his admission is academic and formal, not moral and spiritual. He is a hypocrite . . . .

The Two Kinds of Truth

Since "being" is the subject of any investigation, philosophers never quibble over the fact that the real is the true. One may say, for example, "This is truly a pleasant afternoon," or, "This is truly part of the American way of life." Whatever is, is true. To the extent that something participates in being, it is true. This is called *ontological truth*.

Were there no more to the problem than mere academic agreement on the proposition "The real is the true," philosophers would never wrangle about truth. No matter what the stuff of reality is, it has being, and to this degree it is true.

But how can reality be known? How can we critically distinguish reality from appearance? If ontological truth is to be of any service, therefore, a procedure must be devised that will put man's mind in touch with reality. This procedure is rational inference. Whenever a person enters a new environment, he is compelled to make inferences, for man is curious by nature. Symbols or terms represent concepts, and the valid construing of these symbols is truth. *Propositional truth,* thus, is the second kind of truth. Whenever judgments conceptually house the real, they possess the quality of truth.

It makes no difference whether ideas *are* the real, or whether they *correspond* to the real. In either instance the

[1] Oliver Goldsmith, *The Vicar of Wakefield* (Oxford), p. 32.

proposition is the receptacle of truth. Nor is it of any moment how particular philosophers verify propositional truth: whether by the power of propositions to guide our experience without frustration (systematic consistency); by the correspondence of ideas to things (correspondence); by the consistency of ideas with each other (coherence); or by operational differences in controlled experiment (pragmatism). Whatever the stripe of a philosopher may be, he still has to think, and in thinking he must make inferences. The manner of his life proves that the proposition is the cradle of truth.

With the rarest exceptions — such as Socrates, Pascal, and Kierkegaard — thinkers have rather consistently confined themselves to a defense of these two kinds of truth. Such a restriction, I assert, is a fruit of philosophy's dreadful habit of ignoring the moral and spiritual realities that already hold man as a creature made in the image of God.

The Third Kind of Truth

It is no simple task to unmask the deficiency of classical philosophy, however, for its error is more one of omission than of commission. I am fully persuaded that if one criticizes philosophy's passion to be precise in either ontological or propositional truth, he simply shows his own want of good sense. Were classical philosophy to be judged by its devotion to the conventional kinds of truth, we would have to doff our hats in praise. Reality is the "given" in truth, while experience and judgment make it possible for the whole man to contact reality.

But what if a third kind of truth exists, one that is the precise equivalent of neither ontological nor propositional truth? What if there were a kind of truth which, in Kierkegaard's words, "comes into being" only as one is transformed by ethical decision? Philosophers think that when they have developed an elaborate system of propositional truth, they can rest on their laurels, quite content that the task is finished. But if Socrates and Kierkegaard are right, such a retirement is culpably premature. The *real* business of philosophy has not even started.

By the term "third kind of truth" I mean *truth as personal rectitude*. The possibility of rectitude is implied in the very meaning of moral freedom itself, for uprightness does not come into being until man as he is coincides with man as he ought to be. For example, if one ought to be transformed by the fact that he is dependent on powers greater than himself, truth as personal rectitude has no existence until one morally and spiritually conforms the whole of his life to this relation. Essence and existence are united by right moral decision. If one chooses to scorn this responsibility, the third type of truth is shorn of reality.

Since man is part of nature, and yet enjoys moral freedom over nature, it is easy to suppose that man's affinity with nature invests him with the same harmony that is enjoyed by a flower. Let us call man's natural features the "descriptive essence." This essence takes in all that belongs to man as he is: legs, organs, reproductive desires, and so on. Viewed from the perspective of his descriptive essence, man really and truly is; existence and essence are federated harmoniously.

Unlike brutes, however, man remains spiritually free to make or undo the most important aspect of his being. Men have moral freedom; they are entrusted with the responsibility of creating or destroying rectitude by the quality of their own decisions. Let us call the stuff of rectitude the "imperative essence." Even as the descriptive essence comprehends all that man is, so the imperative essence comprehends all that man ought to be. Moral and spiritual decision cannot be shunned without deteriorating character, for essence and existence are not in harmony until one elects to live uprightly.

The Two Conventional Methods of Knowing

If the fulfillment of duty is man's most important responsibility, however, one would think that classical philosophy would have devoted its best talents to devising a method which answers the question, "How is a knowledge of the imperative essence possible?" But this certainly has not been the case. Just as it has been assumed that there are only two types of truth — ontological and propositional — so it has been assumed that there are only two methods of knowing: knowledge by acquaintance and knowledge by inference. Let us briefly review these two types of knowing, showing why neither is able to lead the mind into a conceptual awareness of the imperative essence. If one expects to grasp the third type of truth — truth as personal rectitude — he must develop a theory of knowledge which can make peace with the data of the moral and spiritual environment.

Knowledge by acquaintance is the passage of the mind to a conclusion without the aid of a middle premise. Acquaintance is direct experience. For example, when Thomas De Quincey tried to tell what it meant to bask in the ecstasy of opium, precise words failed him. His experience paragoned description. "Eloquent opium! that with thy potent rhetoric stealest away the purposes of wrath, pleadest effectually for relenting pity, and through one night's heavenly sleep callest back to the guilty man the visions of his infancy, and hands washed pure from blood."[2] Intimate emotions, such as love, joy, and grief, are effectively known only as they are felt. The same is true about the more universal aspects of nature. For example, Samuel Johnson wisely observes that though we *know* what light is, it is not easy to *tell* what light is. Augustine said the same thing about the meaning of time.

Knowledge by acquaintance answers to ontological truth. If one wants to know the sunset in all its presentational immediacy, he must face the west and open his eyes. He must experience the sunset. Since whatever is, is true, and since experience is our only way of apprehending the wholeness of what is, it follows that only knowledge by acquaintance can directly apprehend ontological truth. A child defines a cat by pointing at it. Since he experiences the cat, he knows the cat.

Knowledge by inference is the passage of the mind to a conclusion with the aid of a middle premise.[3] The syllogism is the foundation of valid inference: "All men are mortals; Socrates is a man; therefore, Socrates is a mortal." Valid inference can be simple or complex, but it must always follow the rules of logic. Knowledge by inference begins with simple judgment — "This is a horse" — and it ends with vast libraries of ponderous tomes. A system of thought is the consummate fruit of human reflection. But systems must be reflected on; they cannot be directly intuited.

Nothing will be gained by laboring this. It is sufficient to note that whenever a judgment is formed about the real, the thinker relies on rational inference to acquaint his mind with truth. If an expert geologist makes a series of judgments about the meaning of certain rock strata, his inferences are valid if they place the mind in contact with the real. This, quite obviously, is why knowledge by inference answers to truth as

[2] *Confessions of an English Opium-Eater* (Oxford), p. 217.

[3] In broadest terms, of course, *all* knowledge is inferential. Knowledge by acquaintance completes the inference without a middle premise, while knowledge by inference does not. Let us not be confused. We have simply distinguished these two species of inference in order that our efforts may enjoy greater precision.

propositional correspondence to reality. A valid inference always yields a true conclusion — providing it is based on true premises.

But if knowledge by acquaintance directly introduces the mind to reality, while knowledge by inference houses the real by means of symbols and words, what method escorts the mind into the imperative essence? How can we grasp the nature of that one species of being which has no existence until free, moral decision closes the gap between what an individual is and what he ought to be? That is the problem . . . .

[*Following a discussion of the limitations of both knowledge by acquaintance and knowledge by inference, Carnell turns to what he calls the third method of knowing.*]

The Third Method of Knowing

Since man enjoys veto rights over his own impulses, one can only know the content of the imperative essence by a total spiritual acceptance of the duties to which he is already committed by existence itself.[4] Rather than experientially or speculatively fingering mere claims to duty, one must allow himself to be transformed by the duties that hold him as he drives his car or shops for a new furnace.

Man is a spiritual creature; praiseworthy moral decision forms the very essence of his dignity. But if one will not spiritually acquaint himself with the components of his moral life, nothing from the outside can move him — whether it be a system of ethics, a self-transcendent survey of his own impulses, or a scientific review of how men conduct themselves in other cultures. The obligation to meet duty is part of duty. Duty can never be measured by thought; its essence eludes detection until one is morally and spiritually controlled by a sense of duty.

This is why I assert that a knowledge of the imperative essence will never be felt until one places himself in the

[4] This expression, "the duties to which he is already committed by existence itself," will doubtless sound gratuitous and naive to the reader. How does "existence itself" establish a line of argument from a person reared on Christian soil to a German conditioned by Hitler? Of what value, then, is an appeal to duties that already hold us? I have no other response than that I am conscious of these problems and that in due time I shall give my attention to them.

center of those obligations which form the moral and spiritual environment of his life. If he shrinks from this, preferring to deal with either rational or empirical claims to duty, he will never move one inch toward a correct knowledge of the imperative essence.

But what name shall I give the third method of knowing, in order that it may henceforth be referred to with convenience and accuracy? Let us remember that terms are only useful; they cannot be true or false. A name is serviceable to the degree that it accurately denotes the ideas one has in mind. I shall call the third method of knowing *knowledge by moral self-acceptance.* The content of the imperative essence cannot be apprehended until one is spiritually transformed by the sum of those duties which already hold him . . . . Although knowledge by acquaintance and knowledge by inference are the only ways in which the content of the imperative essence can be brought before the mind, only moral self-acceptance can release the data which make up this essence. If a person will not submit to the moral sense, he will remain spiritually blind; for neither acquaintance nor inference has access to the pith and marrow of the imperative essence. Only moral self-acceptance can release a sense of duty into consciousness. Once duty has been released, of course, it then can be directly experienced or conceptually represented . . . .

It is important to notice how Wisdom answers one who acts rashly, for Wisdom's word may resolve our difficulty. Anxious to save one from the effect of his own imprudence, it says, "Why, you know better than that!" Foolish conduct is a sin against knowledge. To say that an individual "knows" better is merely another way of saying that he is responsible for acquainting himself with the outcome of his choices. And this is precisely what is meant by the third condition of knowing: *To know is to be morally responsible for knowing.* Although one does not meet the first condition of knowing until he experiences something, and although one does not meet the second condition of knowing until he reasons consistently, one already meets the third condition of knowing by virtue of his being a normal human being. Moral responsibility is the third condition of knowing. A person must spiritually anticipate the outcome of his actions . . . .

Preparations for Meeting God

If one were content to know the *existence* of God, rather than pressing on to an acquaintance with God's *person*, this would be the logical place for him to stop; for the probe from here on will seem pointless to all who do not appreciate the fact that personality can only be known as one either introduces himself or is introduced. If we want to enjoy a rich knowledge of God, deliberate steps must be taken to become acquainted with His person. To refuse acquaintance is to refuse knowledge. An inferential knowledge of God's existence is without value until fellowship is gained by an acquaintance with God's person. In person-to-person relations, knowledge by inference must yield to knowledge by acquaintance .... [An intellectual love of God is not sufficient.] The real man is not the rational man; the real man is the moral and the loving man .... Until fellowship with God is enjoyed, it is clear that we do not rightly know God.

Extending the Cycle of Fellowship

From the very beginning I have argued that the nearness of God makes it difficult to develop a perspective from which to decide what conditions must be met if we are to enjoy fellowship with God. Such a difficulty is clearly illustrated at this point in the argument. How can we go about acquainting ourselves with the person of God? Where shall we begin?

At an earlier point we asked the question, "Under what conditions shall we trust another individual?" And we answered, "We shall trust him only to the extent that he shows signs of receiving the dignity of our person." This query led to what we called the "cycle of fellowship": an introductory word, the sustained pleasure, and a warm gesture of farewell. Let us now extend this cycle by adding a new element.

Suppose we are walking along the bank of a muddy river, when suddenly we notice that a young mother's rowboat has slipped its knot and is drifting out into the current. Without calculating consequences, we dash into the water and reach for the line, only to soak our clothing and be inconvenienced for the rest of the day. When we finally recover the boat and return it to the woman, does our participation in the moral and spiritual environment oblige her to meet any new terms?

There can be no doubt, as we ponder this and similar illustrations, that *whenever we do a large favor for another, the person helped is morally obligated to express a spontaneous word of thanks.* By *large* we mean measurable, out of the way, not legally expected. Whoever is faithful to the manner of his own life will immediately recognize that there is no exception to this rule. *Not* to look for evidences of spontaneous gratitude is as clear a sign of character deterioration as an indifference either to one's own dignity or to the moral demand that others respect it . . . .

The sum of the matter is this: if we expect to approach the person of God, our effort will be presumptuous unless we are held by spontaneous feelings of gratitude for all God has done. This much is clear. But words of gratitude can only be exchanged within fellowship itself. So, this leaves us just about where we started. An enlargement of the cycle of fellowship has solved no problems. Our plight, in fact, has even worsened. The more we know about the good, the less able we are to be good.

Spiritual Preparation and the Perception of Truth

Classical thought has seldom appreciated the fact that one can "know" another person only after definite spiritual preparation. Philosophers assume that, regardless of what phase of reality one may probe, the preparations for knowledge are quite the same. This simply is not true.

Take the trivial matter of knowing a pear, for example. There are at least three different approaches to the pear, each requiring a different quality of preparation: Is it a pear? How does the pear taste? May I take the pear? Knowledge by inference establishes the reality of the pear; knowledge by acquaintance the taste; and knowledge by moral self-acceptance our ethical relation to the pear. If a person confuses this order, he confuses knowledge; and if he negates any one method he negates his chances of knowing a part of reality. Knowledge by inference answers to mind; knowledge by acquaintance answers to perceptive faculties; and knowledge by moral self-acceptance answers to the moral sense. Rational inference may decide the existence of the pear, but it cannot tell how a pear tastes; and general experience may decide the taste, but it cannot tell whether it is right to make off with the pear. Each method answers to some specific aspect of man, and this aspect, in turn, answers to the whole individual.

As we shift from one method of knowing to the next, a shift must likewise be made in the spiritual tone of the heart. And just as there are three methods of knowing — each answering to a particular aspect of the real — so there are three grades of spiritual preparation.

Knowledge by inference asks for nothing but a desire to construe one's judgments consistently. This calls for a modicum of spiritual preparation, but the amount is too insignificant to be identified. An arrogant individual can excel in logic and mathematics. Perhaps this is why philosophers restrict themselves to knowledge by inference, for pride is left untouched.

Knowledge by acquaintance asks one to relate the content of experience to what he publicly professes. Since one can easily deny what he experiences, a measure of real humility is presupposed. The less public the data are, the more convenient it is for ignorance and pride to deny them. A guilty person can stand before the court and plead, "Not guilty." A severely injured person can reply, "Pain has no reality; it is an error of the material sense." Because knowledge by acquaintance asks for a correlation of experience and profession, it calls for much greater spiritual preparation than knowledge by inference.

Knowledge by moral self-acceptance asks for a spiritual willingness to be morally transformed by the realities that already hold one. The content of experience must be related to the total self, not simply to what one professes. Thus, the spiritual preparation is the greatest. The third species of truth — truth as personal rectitude — has no existence until one closes the gap between what he is and what he ought to be. The whole person must be spiritually drawn into the task. This means that one cannot even begin the third method of knowing until he has won a decided spiritual victory in his heart. One will not recognize the content of the moral and spiritual environment until he is humble, for duty is not known until one stands within the center of duty.

No profound truth can be perceived until all three methods are effectively blended. One cannot say, "I know my neighbor," let alone, "I know God," until he submits to the witness of the fourfold environment — physical, rational, aesthetic, and moral and spiritual. To know a friend calls for the verdict of sense perception ("the friend is warm"), the faculty of judgment ("the friend is Norwegian"), and the moral sense ("the friend is kind"). The assertion, "This is my friend," cannot be established either by logic or by science. There is no straight-line way to prove the reality of personality. Even as others do not know us until they are humble, so we do not know others until we are humble. The meaning of personality must be spiritually intuited. Whenever one attempts to establish our reality by speculative techniques, he arouses the judicial sentiment and we judge him guilty. He is guilty because he violates the claims of the moral and spiritual environment. He has no right to treat us as an object.

If we cannot approach one another without satisfying the claims of the moral and spiritual environment, how can we avoid these claims when approaching God? Is it easier to know God than a fellow citizen? We certainly dare not treat God as an object; He cannot be regarded as the conclusion to a rational argument. God must be spiritually experienced; He must be encountered in the dynamic of fellowship.

God, it seems, is always just beyond the reach of our interests. Although the dignity of our life is safeguarded by the divine vigil, we tend to transact all business in the impersonal corridors of the judicial sentiment. After the dignity of our lives has been vindicated, rather than seeking out God and thanking Him, we turn to other interests.

Since it is advantageous to have God complete the moral cycle by answering to the judicial sentiment, it might appear that we are guilty of using God as a means to our own calculated ends. But such is not the case. Although we look to God to complete the moral cycle, we are held in this necessity from existence itself. Since we are made in God's image, we cannot be indifferent to those who abuse us. We can more easily flee from the universe than we can flee from the presence of God, for in Him we live and move and are. "If I ascend to heaven, thou art there! If I make my bed in Sheol, thou art there! If I take the wings of the morning and dwell in the uttermost parts of the sea, even there thy hand shall lead me, and thy right hand shall hold me" (Ps. 139:8-10). Therefore, if the charge of culpability is to be leveled anywhere, this is not the place. God has made certain that the whole human race shall look to Him for spiritual as well as physical and rational well-being.

Some might despair of ever enjoying fellowship with God. They err. We *know* the preconditions of fellowship because we are morally *responsible* for knowing — thus decrees the third condition of knowing, a condition that holds us from existence itself. Since we are able to discover that God is a person, we are equally able to discover the terms of fellowship; for the second piece of information is analytically implied in the first. If one admits that God is a person, but despairs of ever knowing God through acquaintance, he contradicts himself.

The Moral Predicament

From the very beginning we have admitted that we depend on powers greater than ourselves. These powers, we now know, center in God. All we have and are is a gracious gift. "What have you that you did not receive? If then you received it, why do you boast as if it were not a gift?" (I Cor. 4:7). Even our ability to strive and get gain is from God. Without Him we can do nothing. "Beware lest you say in your heart, 'My power and the might of my hand have gotten me this wealth.' You shall remember the Lord your God, for it is he who gives you power to get wealth; that he may confirm his covenant which he swore to your fathers, as at this day" (Deut. 8:17-18). This means that if we fail to be held by spontaneous sentiments of gratitude toward God, we sin.

Since this is the case, it would seem that we ought to get on with it. But this is easier said than done. Though we may sincerely *want* to be held by expressions of gratitude for all God has done, we have no power to make good this intention. We simply cannot convert our affections. "Can the Ethiopian change his skin or the leopard his spots? Then also you can do good who are accustomed to do evil" (Jer. 13:23). The more we consciously strive to arouse sentiments of spontaneous gratitude, the more we are betrayed into what I call a "moral predicament." Each effort to escape this predicament draws us all the more deeply into it. We are like wretches in a pool of quicksand: our very determination to escape lowers us all the deeper into the liquid death.

Here is a pithy summary of the moral predicament: *Although it is evil to be morally indifferent to those who do us favors, not only are we held by a spontaneous sense of gratitude when we contemplate the divine favors, but we have insufficient moral resources to convert ourselves.* The more we *try* to be grateful, the more affected, and thus the less moral, our attitude becomes. We may wring our hands, meditate with our faces toward heaven, or drone out holy desires to have fellowship with God; but at the end of each religious exercise we end as spectators who acknowledge a moral task greater than we can meet. We cannot thank God unless we have fellowship with God; but our very want of thankfulness is itself a barrier to fellowship. Which way can we turn?

It would be very easy for one to *pretend* that he has feelings of spontaneous gratitude to God, but this surely would conduce to folly. "If we say we have no sin, we deceive ourselves, and the truth is not in us" (I John 1:8). Carlyle observes, in this connection, that the greatest of faults is to be conscious of none. Since an omniscient God forms the environment in which man lives and moves and is, holy eyes scrutinize our every thought and intention. "O Lord, thou hast searched me and known me! Thou knowest when I sit down and when I rise up; thou discernest my thoughts from afar. Thou searchest out my path and my lying down, and art acquainted with all my ways" (Ps. 139:1-3). A resolution to be transparently honest before God may not secure fellowship, but it at least provides a clean moral platform on which to build. We cannot deceive God.

I must confess that no fruit of the third method of knowing has proved more puzzling than the moral predicament. We admit we ought to be held by spontaneous sentiments of gratitude, yet we have no moral resources to convert ourselves. If we were grateful by nature, we would fulfill rectitude out of unconscious necessity.

The moral predicament is serious because it throttles the very possibility of fellowship. Fellowship is a daughter of spiritual spontaneity; it is not brought into being by legal or rational striving. But until we are personally acquainted with God, we really do not know God, for personality must be experienced to be known.

Although we speak of God as "personal," William James would be quick to point out that, functionally and pragmatically, we *mean* the same thing that Aristotle meant by the unmoved mover. God is an ultimacy who explains areas in our life that we happen to call important. We postulate God to explain our participation in the moral and spiritual environment, while Aristotle postulated God to explain motion and rest in nature. But what is the functional difference between these two efforts? Until we know God by acquaintance, there is none.

The Character of God

One phase of the moral predicament must now be carefully examined, for it may help us resolve our difficulty. Suppose the moral predicament *does* exist. Are we culpable for this fact? Can we be blamed for failing in what we cannot do? Blind people cannot see color, and we cannot arouse spontaneous sentiments of gratitude; but may either of us be meaningfully blamed? It would seem not.

As I meditated further, I discovered that an important phase of our relation to God has not yet been explored. What if it can be shown that God completes the moral cycle from a necessity that is immanent in His own character? Would this not immediately relieve the moral predicament? Just as God exists of necessity,[5] so He completes the moral cycle of necessity; and just as we need not thank God for His existence, so we need not thank Him for completing the moral cycle. If this accords with truth, the case is closed.

Some may charge us with probing into the secret things of God: "We have no present right to look into God's essence, for the privilege is reserved for the beatific vision. We must *believe,* not question." This is all well and good, but what should we believe? Unless we can spell out the terms of fellowship, we cannot prepare to meet God.

The truth is, we already know the essence of God. God is perfect rectitude. God unfailingly defends our dignity by answering to the judicial sentiment. To argue otherwise would be repugnant to truth. Were we to assert that God is *not* held by a necessity to judge those who mistreat us, we would obscure the clearest element in our moral experience; for our reliance on God is woven into the very fabric of existence itself. It is impossible to have fellowship with wicked people. But it is not we who judge the wicked; it is God who judges them through us. We are only vessels through which a duly authorized moral tribunal works. We have no native rights to judge one another. "For there is no authority except from God" (Rom. 13:1). This is why we cannot avoid believing that God completes the moral cycle out of a necessity that resides in His own character. We are only saying, in more elaborate language, that God is God. God and an upright man are held by similar attitudes toward justice and injustice, for the moral and spiritual environment is common to both. The more perfect man is, the more like God he becomes.

But some may ask, "Are we not limiting God? Isn't a sovereign God free to do whatever He wants?" Certainly God is free — absolutely free. Freedom means that one acts in accord with his nature; and it *is* in accord with God's nature to see the

[5] In asserting that God exists of necessity, we are not appealing to the ontological argument. Kierkegaard has given the *coup de grâce* to the Anselmic dream of passing from the idea of God to the existence of God. (See Kierkegaard, *Concluding Unscientific Postscript* [Princeton University Press], p. 298.) We here argue from within the Thomistic-Kantian tradition. If *anything* exists, something exists of necessity. This necessity is God. The argument from contingency is dialectically more compelling than that drawn from the idea of an all-perfect being.

judgment of those who abuse us. This in no way impedes sovereignty.

It is not we who limit God, but God who limits our power of apprehending Him. We perceive God in and through the claims of the moral and spiritual environment, for we live and move and are in God.

Others may add, "But if we cannot trust a fellow human unless he shows signs of receiving our dignity, neither can we trust God unless He shows similar signs; in which case we place an abstract rule above God, and God is no longer sovereign." The objection fails to respect our true relation to God. We do not turn God's standards back on God, for it is God Himself who judges immoral people through us. A house divided against itself cannot stand. Were it not that we live and move and are in God, we should never know what duty is. We should be brutes. Dissolve our confidence that God completes the moral cycle, and the very meaning of rectitude collapses.

The moral and spiritual environment admits of no exceptions. Whenever a person enters the circle of nearness — be he God or man — we *cannot* extend fellowship until he shows signs of receiving the dignity of our person. This necessity is not subject to the control of our will, for we are held by an a priori expectation. But this expectation in no way justifies the charge that we judge God by a standard higher than God. A discriminating mind will see that when we look to God for evidences that He is God, we are already piously submitting to God; for God Himself, as we have shown, makes up the claims of the moral and spiritual environment. *This means that the character of God is the norm by which we test for the character of God.* If a cosmic being appeared before us, but showed no signs of truth and justice, we would know that he was not God. The devil is the father of all lies. False religions deserve their title because they appeal to a supreme being whose character is not continuous with the claims of the moral and spiritual environment.

Christian theologians are usually more chary of this structure than secular philosophers. This is explained by their zeal to safeguard the sovereignty of God. I commend them in this, for their caution reflects a genuine respect for the divine integrity. But their attitude ceases to be praiseworthy when it dulls the mind to see and defend truth. Suppose a religious prophet said, "God delights in those who commit murder." Would a morally upright theologian assign this to God? The answer is plain. He would not because he could not, and he could not because the claims of the moral and spiritual environment would be violated. This shows that the theologian, down deep in his heart, really believes the position we are defending. And believing it, he ought to acknowledge it.

Thus, it is wide of the mark to say that we judge God by a rule that is metaphysically more ultimate than God. We test for God to be sure, but God Himself is the author of our expectation that God will show signs of rectitude. If one looks to fellowship with God, he must know what kind of evidences to expect when God reveals Himself. A moral man honors God by resolutely refusing to worship non-God. Plato elevated the Good above God, but the Christian does not. The Christian judges God by God.

This accounts for both the purity of the standard and our immutable right to apply it. Those who mistreat us are guilty; this is a moral absolute. Night or day, now or at the hour of our death, we are calmly confident that God answers to the judicial sentiment by a necessity that is immanent in His own character. We are relieved of any fear that the intrinsic value of our life will be revised in the light of shifting standards, for the character of God is the fixed point for defining our spiritual dignity. Were it not for this unassailable truth, the meaning of decency would immediately collapse.

One is not rightly related to God, and thus does not rightly know God, unless he recognizes that the very character of God issues in a moral guardianship of those who are made in His image. Either we ground our hope in the person of God, or we are betrayed into a capital error from the very start.

Rather than unworthily intruding into the counsels of God, therefore, our contention that God necessarily defends human dignity is simply another way of saying that God is God. He is perfectly held by the same moral necessities that hold an upright man imperfectly. Rectitude consists in a spontaneity that is unconscious of lawful necessity; and God enjoys perfect rectitude.

If we cannot believe that our dignity is grounded in God, there is no way of disproving the extreme charge that man's moral standards are so different from those of God that what man calls good, God calls bad. In this event, our very effort to clarify the relation between time and eternity would be nullified. We would be agnostic regarding the divine standards. It would be meaningless to speak of "moral preconditions when approaching God," for we would be devoid of any norm by which to anticipate the nature of such conditions.

One may strongly disagree with what William Ellery Channing finally did with his assertion, but it is difficult to deny the truth of the assertion itself; namely, that if we have no moral equipment with which to judge what agrees or disagrees with the character of God, then what we *think* is consistent with perfect rectitude may, when the scrolls of eternity are unrolled, be found consistent with malignity and error.

But back to what originally brought on this discussion. Let us not lose sight of the problem before us. We inquired whether we might be relieved of the moral predicament on the ground that God must defend our dignity out of a necessity that is immanent in His own character. Having shown that it is both spiritually decorous and rationally consistent to believe that God *does* defend our lives out of such a necessity, we may now proceed with the question: "Does this necessity relieve us of the moral predicament?"

When one judges the issue by the third method of knowing, the answer is decidedly in the negative. Even though an act of kindness is performed out of necessities that flow from moral character itself, the one benefited is in no way exempt from the necessity of expressing spontaneous feelings of gratitude. Suppose we risk our lives to save a friend from a burning building. Although we are borne along by uncalculated, spontaneous courage, this absence of forecast in no way nullifies the fact that, at a convenient moment, a word of gratitude must be given. And if such an expression is not forthcoming — when opportunities to do so exist — the one we have rescued is culpable.

There is no reason to believe that any other principle holds in the case of our relation to God. Even though God completes the moral cycle by a necessity that is immanent in His own character, we are morally culpable if we fail to be held by spontaneous sentiments of gratitude for all God has done. And so, we are cast back on the moral predicament; for even though we may desire to be held by a natural love for God we lack the power to convert ourselves. We are not free, for there is discord in our affections.

The Univocal Point of Identity Between Time and Eternity

Although the problem of time and eternity is common to both philosophy and theology, the labors of the theologians are generally less profound than those of the philosophers. This is due to their refusal to acknowledge a univocal point of identity between time and eternity. The theologians make two separate mistakes. They err in thinking that the problem of time and eternity *can* be solved without affirming a point of identity, and they err in thinking that the affirming of such a point would either anthropomorphize God or deify man.

Since man is made in the image of God, man shares in the life of God whenever he makes contact with ultimate elements in either the rational, aesthetic, or moral and spiritual environment.[6] The true, the beautiful, and the good find their metaphysical status in God. And man comprehends each sphere through a specific point of contact: the law of contradiction, the law of proportion, and the law of life respectively. God is truth; God is beauty; and God is love. But since the third method of knowing has restricted itself to the claims of the moral and spiritual environment, it is only right, in the interests of economy, that we limit our inquiry to this one point of contact.

We may conceive of this point of contact in either the *broad* or the *narrow* sense. The total claims of the moral and spiritual environment make up the broad point of contact between God and man, for God Himself forms the very stuff of this environment. The narrow point of contact is the judicial sentiment. It is narrow because it focuses our attention on one particularly pure aspect of the moral transaction between God and man. And because it is narrow, it is also more precise. Once we see why the judicial sentiment is the point of contact in the narrow sense, we shall also see why the moral and spiritual environment is the point of contact in the broad sense.

The judicial sentiment is the guardian of our dignity. When right moral conditions prevail and our life is respected, it blends into the background and is dormant. But when our dignity is violated, it rushes forward to defend the life. It remains rigidly alert until the offending party propitiates it

[6] We omit the physical environment because it is the field on which elements in the other environments express themselves. For example, by our transcendental participation in the law of proportion, we perceive beauty in nature: and this perception, in some way, is a perception of God. Knowing God, we are reminded of Him in nature. Cf. Psalm 19:1 and Romans 1:20. At this point Plato and the Pythagoreans were not far from the kingdom. Augustine properly affirms that not only is God the light by which we see truth, but He is also the truth seen. [See Ronald H. Nash, *The Light of the Mind: St. Augustine's Theory of Knowledge* (University of Kentucky Press, 1969).]

by meeting the right moral conditions. We have no active part in either the arousing or the subduing of the judicial sentiment. The entire transaction occurs without authorization from our will. The judicial sentiment is deaf to everything but an immoral act. We have no power to awaken it, and we have no power to placate it. This is only to say, as we have said before, that valid judgment of another life is the judgment of God working through us. Whoever offends the image of God offends God. Only God can judge, and only God can forgive. This is why the judicial sentiment is our most precise point of contact between time and eternity. A man is in contact with God, and thus should acknowledge it, whenever he entertains an aroused judicial sentiment; for the voice of the judicial sentiment is the voice of God. The significance of this will develop as we proceed.

This justifies a further word about Christ's counsel, "Judge not, that you be not judged." An aroused judicial sentiment, when morally pure, is not our own judgment; it is God judging others through us. Hence, the counsel of Christ is not offended until we sully the purity of the judicial sentiment by unlovely feelings. But the moment we do this, we become sinners; for we try to complete the moral cycle without help from God. Either we wait on God to complete this cycle, or we violate rectitude. And there are three ways — and only three — that God does this. First, by our going to the offending party and in a friendly tone asking him to apologize. Second, by summoning a duly appointed officer. Third, by submitting to the ambiguity of history and waiting for the final judgment. But sinners are tempted to reject all three alternatives. Suppose they have been offended while riding in their car. First, they are too cowardly to confront the other driver. Second, the incident is too small to be reported to an officer. Third, they are too anxious for settlement to wait for the final judgment. So, they take the law into their own hands. They think or say unkind things about the other driver. At this instant they violate the counsel of Christ, for they usurp a prerogative that belongs to God alone.

I am not unfamiliar with the clamant protests of those who say that if God and man have anything in common, the Creator-creature relation is effaced and God no longer rules man with a sovereignty that is metaphysically discontinuous with creation. But do these zealots realize what they are asserting? Unless God and man have something in common, it is impossible to make meaningful judgments about God.

Hence, if one elects to guard God's sovereignty by denying that God and man share some point of identity, he should prepare for the fact that nothing significant can be known or said about God—not even that there is a God, let alone that God is a person. God and man cannot meaningfully be compared unless they have something in common. This is true of all analogies. If we say, "The mind is to the soul as the eye is to the body," the univocal element is "light" or "guide." And if we say, "A steamship is like a canoe," the univocal element is "force-propelled conveyance for water transport." But what element could God and man possibly have in common, save the moral and spiritual environment?

And when I say common, I mean common, for the issue is too critical to be obscured by a slippery use of language. *I now mean, even as I shall continue to mean, that the moral and spiritual environment on the finite level is precisely of the same stuff as the moral and spiritual environment on the divine level; and that it is not improper to say that God is perfectly held by standards that hold an upright man imperfectly.*[7] God's moral nature issues in a praise of the good and a condemnation of the bad; and so does that of an upright man. God defends justice and condemns injustice; and so does an upright man. "Thus says the Lord God: Enough, O princes of Israel! Put away violence and oppression, and execute justice and righteousness; cease your evictions of my people, says the Lord God. You shall have just balances, a just ephah, and a just bath" (Ezek. 45:9-10). This is only another way of saying that God and an upright man share the same moral and spiritual environment. When our affections are transformed by the claims of this environment, we become good. But God is good by nature.

I realize how blasphemous this will sound to those who cower before Feuerbach's charge that man has made God in his own image and that all theology is nothing but anthropology. I can only say, in reply, that it is foolish to correct one error by introducing a new one. If the meaning of God's character cannot be anticipated by information drawn from our own conception of decency, what significance is conveyed by the term "God"? And how can God be distinguished from other unknowables? These are extremely serious problems.

[7] This is only a manner of speaking, of course, for the divine life confronts no outside environment. An upright man completes his life in God, while God completes His life in Himself. God is held by affections that inhere in His own character. But this distinction in no way alters the truth that God and an upright man have identical attitudes toward good and evil, justice and injustice.

Our position does not imply pantheism. We speak only of a common *environment*, not a common essence. Beings of incompatible orders can share the same environment without sharing the same essence, as when human beings and brutes breathe the same air. Man's essence consists in personality expressed through moral and rational self-transcendence, while that of the brute does not. God is uncreated, self-generating essence, while man is created, dependent essence. Yet, both share the same moral and spiritual environment. Man lives, and moves, and is in God. The defense of life, and the condemnation of those who mistreat it, are spontaneous moral sentiments that make up the characters of both God and an upright man. The third method of knowing safeguards God's transcendence not only by showing that creation is dependent on God for its being, but also by showing that creation is judged by a norm that flows from the very substance of the divine character.

Since man lives and moves and is in God, at least two analogical predications about God can be made. First, "God is a person." A person, let us recall, is "freedom expressed through moral self-consciousness." Second, "God praises justice and condemns injustice out of a necessity that resides in His own character."

If modern theologians would only heed the realities that already hold them, they would immediately perceive that most of the debate about "point of contact" is merely sophomoric quibbling. God is "wholly other" only in a very special sense. One cannot even walk down the street without participating in a moral and spiritual environment that is common to both God and an upright man. God is immanent as well as transcendent. Theologians ought to recognize that when others are unkind to them, or when their rights are violated, the judicial sentiment is aroused; and that the judicial sentiment, or analysis, is the voice of a moral tribunal that outreaches human authority. Inconsiderate people are responsible to God. If one nullifies this point of contact, the entire significance of the moral life collapses. Man is left with nothing but tastes and feelings to guide him through social tensions.

Possibly no student of moral philosophy has expressed the matter more effectively than John Stuart Mill. His language is as beautiful as his arguments are persuasive.

> Here, then, I take my stand on the acknowledged principle of logic and of morality, that when we mean different things we

> have no right to call them by the same name, and to apply to them the same predicates, moral and intellectual. Language has no meaning for the words Just, Merciful, Benevolent, save that in which we predicate them of our fellow creatures; and unless that is what we intend to express by them, we have no business to employ the words. If in affirming them of God we do not mean to affirm these very qualities, differing only as greater in degree, we are neither philosophically nor morally entitled to affirm them at all . . . . If in ascribing goodness to God I do not mean what I mean by goodness; if I do not mean the goodness of which I have some knowledge, but an incomprehensible attribute of an incomprehensible substance, which for aught I know may be a totally different quality from that which I live and venerate . . . . what do I mean by calling it goodness? and what reason have I for venerating it? If I know nothing about what the attribute is, I cannot tell that it is a proper object of veneration. To say that God's goodness may be different in kind from man's goodness, what is it but saying, with a slight change of phraseology, that God may possibly not be good? To assert in words what we do not think in meaning, is as suitable a definition as can be given of a moral falsehood. Besides, suppose that certain unknown attributes are ascribed to the Deity in a religion the external evidences of which are so conclusive to my mind as effectually to convince me that it comes from God. Unless I believe God to possess the same moral attributes I find, in however inferior a degree, in a good man, what ground of assurance have I of God's veracity? All trust in a Revelation presupposes a conviction that God's attributes are the same, in all but degree, with the best human attributes.[8]

If David Hume were here to speak, he doubtless would say that our discussion is quite void of meaning. To speak about a "point of contact with God," when we have no information about God, is mere prattle. Since we are empirically closed up to the conditions of time — while God presumably is not — we cannot make meaningful predications about God.

As might be suspected, Hume's difficulty stems from his failure to take a close look at the realities that already hold him from existence itself. The moral and spiritual environment is *not* subject to the limitations of time. It is of the stuff of eternity. Hence, we forthrightly reject the theory of knowledge that inspired Hume's philosophy. We proceed to God by way of an intuitive participation in the moral and spiritual environment, not by way of Lockian percepts. This is an extremely important difference to observe.

[8] *An Examination of Sir William Hamilton's Philosophy* (Longmans, Green and Co.), pp. 127-128.

Others believe that the problems of predication can be solved on the faith that God has authorized a book, church, or priestly caste to witness to His will; and that if one will only submit himself to such authority he will assuredly gain fellowship with God.

The third method of knowing does not for a moment *deny* that God may have elected one, or several, of these means to bridge the gap between time and eternity. This can only be settled by a patient examination of relevant evidences. But if God and man are not analogically related, one can posit as many mediators as he wants, and we yet are left with moral skepticism.

If we submit to a particular book, church, or priestly caste, does it mean that we no longer need to make decisions that decide our destiny? If so, the counsel of Kierkegaard is again germane. Whenever individuals rely on objective security as an escape from moral decision, they jeopardize their own individuality. It would hardly be appropriate to repeat Kierkegaard's incisive arguments here. We need only say, as has been said before, that individuality *consists* in ethical decision; for the real man is the moral man. Neither book, church, nor priestly caste can relieve us of the responsibility of closing the gap between the descriptive essence and the imperative essence; and any attempt to do so would rob us of selfhood.

Or is it meant that if we yield to a book, church, or priestly caste, we shall gain information about God that would otherwise remain inaccessible? If so, it is all the more necessary that the problem of meaningful predication be faced. If we cannot anticipate the character of God by using elements drawn from the moral and spiritual environment, then by the same token we have no way of judging the character of God's representative, since this decision, though one step removed, involves the same difficulty. Unless we can meaningfully anticipate God's standards of rectitude, it may turn out that the book, church, or priestly caste that is least moral on human standards is most moral on divine standards; and we are once again left with skepticism.

Some may rise to a final defense by asserting that it is our religious *duty* to submit to God's representative, whether we understand the reasons or not; for faith is a venture, a leap of the will in the face of paradox and objective uncertainty. To look for evidences is a sign of unbelief. Any delay will only increase our chances of losing eternal happiness.

This is a specious claim. Nothing is our duty unless it is analytically part of a duty to which we are already committed; and in all time it will never be a rational man's duty to submit to demands that outrage larger elements in our fourfold environment—physical, rational, aesthetic, and moral and spiritual. God addresses us as intelligent creatures; His word is never discontinuous with truth . . . .

Moral Self-Acceptance and the Terms of Fellowship

If God and man share the same moral and spiritual environment, not only are we able to make meaningful predications about the divine nature, but we are supplied with a rather decisive way of going about the task of finding fellowship with God.

Since God and man are both persons, it is quite in harmony with good procedure to assert that a knowledge of how to have fellowship with God is analytically included in a knowledge of how men have fellowship with one another. If the moral and spiritual environment joins God and man in one lawful order, then the analogy between God and man ought to hold in all its pivotal points.

Once we approach the question by way of moral self-acceptance, it is not too difficult to name the condition that must be met before fellowship is born. A *person entering the circle of nearness must humble himself.* I do not mean that he must bow and scrape, as if we are his metaphysical superiors. I mean only that we are not at liberty to release the warmth of our personality until he stands in a right relation to the dignity of our lives. Regardless of how willing we may be to extend fellowship, our participation in the moral and spiritual environment makes it impossible to do so until proper moral conditions prevail. A proud and overweening attitude blocks the flow of fellowship as effectively as insulation blocks the flow of electricity.[9]

If this is an accurate representation of truth, it follows that from this point forward we may meaningfully speak of God's self-revelation; for fellowship exists only in revelation. Even as no one can extort fellowship from us (for we share our hearts as a free gift), so we would depart from right procedure if we supposed that one can extort fellowship from God. Fellowship is either cheerfully released or it does not exist at all. There is no third, or middle, condition.

[9] This is not the *only* attitude that blocks fellowship, of course. Modern psychiatry and psychotherapy have found several others. But I choose this one as my paradigm because it most fruitfully gets us on with the job of discovering how to gain fellowship with God. A selection must be made in the interests of economy.

And if humility provides the occasion for men to reveal themselves, humility ought also to provide the occasion for God to reveal Himself. But revelation must come from the divine side; otherwise we shall never have an acquaintance knowledge of God's person.

This leads us back to the meaning of moral rectitude. Whenever others are humble in our presence, and thus meet the terms of fellowship, we become guilty if we refuse to complete the cycle of moral response by revealing ourselves. It is evil to answer humility with pride. Fellowship is a solemn contract; neither party is at liberty to violate its terms without incurring guilt. Just as it is morally wrong to withhold goods from those who have paid for them, so it is morally wrong to withhold fellowship from those who humble themselves. This is clearly proved by the third condition of knowing.

Confident that I have not unduly pressed the univocal point between God and an upright man, I have no hesitation to venture the belief that even as God's character obliges Him to defend the dignity of our lives, so His character obliges Him to reveal Himself whenever the right moral conditions prevail. This will sound blasphemous to those whose theological and apologetical convictions have ossified. But to all who remain docile before the witness of God in the moral and spiritual environment, the assertion is but another way of enforcing the truth that God is God. He enjoys perfect rectitude.

This does not imply that an immanent attribute of benevolence releases God from an interest in the moral condition of those who look to Him for fellowship. To the contrary. Our first encounter with the moral and spiritual environment established God's justice; for God completes the moral cycle by answering to the judicial sentiment. Therefore, *no* man can be received by God until right moral conditions prevail. " 'With what shall I come before the Lord, and bow myself before God on high? Shall I come before him with burnt offerings, with calves a year old? Will the Lord be pleased with thousands of rams, with ten thousands of rivers of oil? Shall I give my first-born for my transgression, the fruit of my body for the sin of my soul?' He has showed you, O man, what is good; and what does the Lord require of you but to do justice, and to love kindness, and to walk humbly with your God?" (Micah 6:6-8). To say that God can have fellowship with those who refuse to humble themselves, what is this but to say that God is not good? Neither God nor an upright man can extend fellowship until right moral conditions prevail.

In sum: *The minimal elements in fellowship oblige us to believe that God is under the same necessity to extend His life to the humble as He is to withhold it from the proud; and that His eternal approval of the humble is but the reverse side of His eternal disapproval of the proud.*[10] "God opposes the proud, but gives grace to the humble" (James 4:6). Our right to believe this stems from the assurance that the claims of the moral and spiritual environment hold both God and man; and that the difference between rectitude in God and rectitude in man is (*mutatis mutandis*) one of degree and not of quantity. God is the standard for measuring rectitude in man. Since we are made in the image of God, we must strive to conform ourselves to the will of God. "You, therefore, must be perfect, as your heavenly Father is perfect" (Matt. 5:48). "You shall be holy, for I am holy" (I Peter 1:16). Such admonitions would be pointless unless God and man shared the same moral and spiritual environment.

If a person shies away from the assertion that a univocal point of identity binds God and an upright man in like attitudes toward justice and injustice, he should prepare to deal with the live rational possibility that God may reveal Himself under conditions that an upright man cannot anticipate — an eventuality that would spell complete moral disaster. If God does not extend fellowship in ways that can be named by a patient study of the manner in which we extend fellowship to one another, we have no sure way of answering those who say that God may confront man on terms that, when judged by our highest norm of rectitude, are contrary to goodness; in which case the lecher and the saint are equal authorities on how an individual may become acquainted with God. Whether men ought to be humble or proud could never be established in advance of the decision.

This seems to clinch the conviction that a refusal to meet the terms of fellowship is the only thing that stands in the way of a reconciliation between God and man.[11] If we fail to enter into fellowship with God, the third condition of

[10] Reasons will be given to show why this assertion gives neither aid nor comfort to the spiritual complacency, "*Dieu pardonnera; c'est son métier.*"

[11] This sweeping universal is premised on information gathered *up to this point*. The reader will err if he thinks this is the whole story. The terms of fellowship are more complex than we may suspect. The cross of Christ stands between sinful man and a holy God. But it would be apologetically imprudent to plunge into this complexity without working up to it by a patient application of the third method of knowing.

knowing warns that the fault is solely ours. We *know* the terms of fellowship because we are morally *responsible* for knowing. "Humble yourselves before the Lord and he will exalt you" (James 4:10). To be humble before God means to conform ourselves to the total fact that He is the sovereign author of all we have and are. Humility is proof that we see and accept this relation.

We can establish the point by a carefully directed application of moral self-acceptance. If we humble ourselves before others, and yet our act is not honored by their release of trust, the judicial sentiment is aroused and we judge them guilty. To refuse to extend fellowship, when the right conditions prevail, is a sure mark of character deterioration.

The Anatomy of Humility

Two things have now been established: first, that humility is the universal precondition of fellowship; second, that although there is no way of measuring quantities of humility, one yet can be confident that if he purifies his affections long enough a place will be reached where fellowship is enjoyed. The problem now is to decide how to go about making ourselves humble.

We cannot become humble by deliberate rational effort, of course, for artificially induced humility is as repugnant to moral self-acceptance as artificially induced gratitude. Nothing is moral unless it freely springs from the imperative essence. Humility before God, like sorrow for acts of evil toward one another, must be a free product of the unfree necessities of the moral and spiritual environment. But what can we do? Shall we simply sit by and wait for God to create feelings of humility in us?

Fearful that this might lead to indolence, I turned to a patient study of the anatomy of humility. At the end of this rewarding probe, I concluded that even as duty is enlarged by showing that new duty is analytically part of a duty already felt, so new experiences of humility can be released from an already existing body of humility. Humility, strangely enough, is its own father and mother. It cannot be sired by either volition or thought. Yet, without both volition and thought one will not place himself in the right condition for humility to extend itself. This is the paradox of humility.

My confidence in asserting this stems from experiences

already reviewed. On at least two separate occasions new humility grew out of a quantity of humility that already held me.

The first experience was honest admission that I am not the author of my own existence. The moment I had the mettle to submit to my own limitations, I was humbled by the realization that I am held by powers over which I have no direct control. Whether I shall continue to live from day to day cannot be established with certainty. The stuff of my existence is very tenuous. "What is your life? For you are a mist that appears for a little time and then vanishes" (James 4:14).

The second experience was a result of the first. The more I contemplated the place of my life in God, the more I recognized that a knowledge of God's benefits does not stir up feelings of spontaneous gratitude in my heart. A submission to the reality of metaphysical dependence made me humble before the reality of the moral predicament.

This was sufficient to assure me that humility is generated by a species of spiritual fission. Although we are powerless to make ourselves humble, we *can* take those steps which release humility into other areas of the life.

Humility increases itself in roughly this order: first, a native willingness to be honest; second, a critical review of the realities that already hold us; third, a moral submission to the claims of these realities. As each new step is taken, the eyes of the understanding behold aspects of the real which remain hidden to pride. Each new insight intensifies our humility. If one will not be honest, he will never recognize that he is a dependent creature; and if he will not submit to the reality of dependence he will never know that he is held by God; and if he will not submit to God he will never know the terms of fellowship. Each submission lays a new deposit of humility on the heart; and these deposits in turn clarify the nature of the real. This again illustrates the truth we have stressed from the beginning: *One cannot perceive ultimates until his affections are in harmony with the moral and spiritual environment.*

Thus, there seems to be no good reason to deny, and several good reasons to affirm, that if we let humility grow by spiritual fission a point would be reached when God would say, "It is enough." If God's character obliges Him to release fellowship whenever proper moral conditions prevail, it would seem that nothing but man's obdurate refusal to meet these conditions stands in the way of our experiencing the person of God. This appeared to be a valid conclusion. In any event, I determined to launch on it until evidences strong enough to challenge its claims could be found.

CHAPTER SEVEN

On Reinhold Niebuhr and Billy Graham

Part One
A Proposal to Reinhold Niebuhr

Reinhold Niebuhr is anxious about Billy Graham. And well he may be, for this young man enjoys no small prestige in modern Christendom. All of us ought to be anxious that Billy Graham will continue to defy the expectation that power corrupts and absolute power corrupts absolutely.

Reinhold Niebuhr is really anxious about orthodoxy in general. But orthodoxy, I find, is not listening. Some conservatives dismiss the anxiety as nothing but personal resentment. Others merely sigh with Beulah-Land detachment, "Billy is *always* charitable to his critics." I believe it would pay orthodoxy to start listening. I also believe it would pay Reinhold Niebuhr to find out why orthodoxy is indifferent.

Here is the pith and marrow of Reinhold Niebuhr's anxiety: Orthodoxy is suspected of departing from the Reformation doctrine that Christians are simultaneously justified and sinful. Billy Graham's departure takes on the form of an easy Christian perfectionism. Observe, for example, his concluding remarks in the film *Eastward to Asia*. If memory serves me well, Billy Graham said something to the effect that "there are no problems facing East and West that Christ cannot solve." Any Christian would accept this in the abstract, of course, for the divine perspective transcends personal interests. But Billy Graham is not talking about the divine perspective. He is cataloguing fruits of personal repentance. The implication is that if a sinner wants to become a skilled diplomat he need only repent.

Such a view of grace is biblically inaccurate. Christ promises forgiveness of sins, not a new endowment for social philosophers. Faith in the cross delivers neither the Christian nor history from the threat of personal preference and biased judgment. When "perfection in Christ" converts to "perfection in the self," those who repent will either magnify what they receive or be disappointed with what they find. The one will lead to pride and the other to pessimism.

Since it tends to obscure the distinction between justification and sanctification, Billy Graham's perfectionism is perilously close to the Roman Catholic doctrine of infused righteousness. Both positions neglect the biblical teaching that sin will tincture man's affections until the resurrection. The Apostle Paul knew, for example, that it was a sin to boast (I Cor. 13:4). Yet he could not disaffiliate himself from the urge to boast (II Cor. 11:16-18; 12:1; etc.). "Another law" wars against the law of the mind. The whole temporal order awaits a work of redemption (Rom. 8:22-25).

The line between the saved and the lost is drawn at the point of forensic justification, not diplomatic ability or inherent moral superiority. It is a stubborn fact — and orthodoxy should come to terms with it — that humanists often develop a finer sense of justice and bear a heavier load of charity than those who profess faith in Christ.

If judicial perfection in Christ and empirical imperfection in the self are not kept in delicate biblical balance, the liberated masses will find it natural to suppose that only a refusal to apply Christian principles prevents them from enjoying immediate justice. Not recognizing the moral limits in their own lives, they will not recognize the moral limits in history. This will breed an impatience with the complex secondary means by which the social order inches its way toward justice. And impatience will breed resentment, and resentment violence.

Reinhold Niebuhr fears that Billy Graham's perfectionism may unwittingly prepare the way for communism. When colonialized people imagine that history can easily overturn injustice they will start asking questions that only communism can answer. Only an atheistic ideology can attack injustice by the use of cynical means — abolition of vested privileges, enforced land reforms, trial without jury. Peter and Paul wisely instructed the Christian slaves to be patient, for injustice would be around for a long time. The apostles knew that unless the slaves recognized the difference between

Christian forgiveness and social justice, pride would use the gospel as an engine of anarchy and revolution.

Having shown why it would pay orthodoxy to listen to Reinhold Niebuhr, let me now show why it would pay Reinhold Niebuhr to find out why orthodoxy is indifferent. The crux of the matter is the rather patronizing way orthodoxy is treated. Rather than being looked on as a serious attempt to mediate the biblical message, it is often dismissed as an anachronistic theological oddity, quite unable to cope with modern problems. Let me make a proposal to Reinhold Niebuhr. I propose that he approach orthodoxy a bit more dialectically.

For example, we hear a resounding "No" to Billy Graham, but the "Yes" is not very distinct. The perils of campaign evangelism should not be understated; neither should they be overstated. Being a minister's son myself, I know a good deal about the less pleasant side of professional soul-winning — the personal strutting, the worldly wisdom, and the theological oversimplification of repentance. But I also know a good deal about the stale churchy formalism and the self-righteous denominationalism which settle on a congregation that is too content with its own procedures to let an outside prophetic voice call sinners to repentance. I think the perennial sickness of Romanism is due in large part to this want of time for personal commitment. The laity attend mass, buy a Sunday newspaper, and then return to their perfunctory life. The church calendar runs full cycle without a call to evangelical repentance. Hatred of Protestants is seldom seriously challenged.

When I was in seminary I was given the impression that moral growth resembles an escalator. Christ comes to maturity in us as we mature to the means of grace. Such a view is only provisionally true. The ordinary means of grace we need, yes. But it so happens that a good deal of our real moral growth comes in a series of spurts. We hear a powerful sermon on purity and we drive a stake in our lives. This in no way nullifies the relevance of future repentance, for spiritual victory always serves as a platform from which to view new heights in Christ. Loving God with our whole heart and our neighbor as ourselves is an infinite progressive task.

It is important to remember that when the apostles preached they preached for decision. And they did not think, as Reinhold Niebuhr seems to think, that decision-preaching is theologically inimical to either the freedom or the necessity of cooperating with non-Christians in mercy and social work.

Reinhold Niebuhr recently proposed that Billy Graham come to terms with the race issue and begin confronting contemporary man with contemporary sins. The proposal was solid, but it was insufficiently dialectical. Not enough allowance was made for the complexity of the problem. Only one-ninth of an iceberg projects above sea level.

I do not think, nor do I think Reinhold Niebuhr really thinks, that Billy Graham would be biblically more accurate if he shifted from individual to collective sins and preached, "Believe on the Lord Jesus Christ, repent of race prejudice, and you will be saved." This would only encourage worldlings to suppose that the really big sin, the one calling for a little "extra" repentance, is racial pride. If a man is busy with the welfare of the Negro he can take a light attitude toward fornication in his own life. Such an outcome would upset the biblical balance just as quickly as Billy Graham's rifle-fire concentration on the "sins of the big city."

Reinhold Niebuhr is supremely right: orthodoxy *must* come to grips with the sin of racial pride. But I do not think this sin should be elevated above the other sins in the apostolic catalogue (Rom. 1:29-31; Gal. 5:19-21; etc.). Too much stress on racial injustice will divert the sinner's attention from the need to repent of his totally self-centered life. Albert Schweitzer has outstripped us all by identifying himself with the misfortunes of the Negro, but this in no way justifies self-righteousness. Unless his sacrifice is a fruit of the Holy Spirit it is done out of pride and profits nothing.

I find it easy to be patient with Billy Graham. Though I have been preaching for many years I have never devoted an entire sermon to the "sins of the white man." And the chief reason for this is my failure to find a final way to measure and defeat racial pride in my own life. It is not easy to preach against oneself. Ministers expose the sins of the laity with great passion and eloquence, but they seldom expose the sins of ministers.

Reinhold Niebuhr's proposal would be more impressive if it were dialectical. It happens that racial injustice has an element of tragedy in it. This tragedy lurks in New York City as well as in the South, for there is still a comfortable physical distance between Harlem and the faculty apartments of Union Theological Seminary. The tragedy is that our desire to actuate the law of love is not matched by the wisdom and virtue needed to succeed. If we pass real-estate zoning laws we do an injustice to the Negro. But if we let the Negro buy a house in a fashionable suburb we do an injustice to vested property interests. With rare exceptions, real estate values are certain to plunge. Hence the tragedy. It is not that we are *unwilling* to do the Christian thing by our brother. The problem is that, being sinners, we are powerless to approach racial injustice from a perspective higher than a prudential balance of personal interests.

Down deep in his heart Billy Graham is just as anxious about racial pride as Reinhold Niebuhr. But my suspicion is that he, like myself, is not quite sure how to go about the matter. The moment one preaches he becomes a hypocrite. One cannot mediate the law until he is subject to the law. Billy Graham feels this insecurity each time he returns to his rather prosperous quarters in the South. The same sense of hypocrisy must arise when he tries to preach against the sins of Houston oil magnates. Scripture says it is wrong for Christians to pay extra attention to the rich (James 2:1-7), but who has moral power to live by this counsel?

If Billy Graham would open his eyes to the reality of the tragic in Billy Graham, he would temper his assertions that repentance yields deposits of wisdom and grace with which to untangle all our difficulties. How can we solve problems confronting East and West when we cannot even solve the problem of justice in real estate zoning?

Let us keep on being anxious — first for ourselves, then for Billy Graham. By keeping this order our anxiety will take on the quality of personal repentance. Unless we sense the ambiguity of sin in our own lives we shall not find it easy to sympathize with the ambiguity of sin in the life of this young evangelist.

The issue, it seems to me, is not whether Billy Graham is always biblically consistent in his preaching. Each of us unconsciously cultivates some heresy or other. The issue is whether Billy Graham is morally uneasy about his inability to be biblically consistent. As long as he is willing to know the right and be transformed by it, Reinhold Niebuhr can ask for nothing more. And the reason he can ask for nothing more is that nothing more can be asked of Reinhold Niebuhr.

Part Two
Can Billy Graham Slay the Giant?

Billy Graham has made elaborate preparations for the New York Campaign. This is only natural, for New York City is the cultural and economic center of the world. It is the home of the Metropolitan Opera and the vast financial interests of Wall Street. Name anything essential to the human venture and it seems that New York City can boast of it in a superlative degree. This complex metropolis is a veritable Goliath. Billy Graham has his sling and his smooth pebbles from the stream, but what are these against the granite towers of Manhattan?

But more exciting for the Christian community, the New York Campaign brings Billy Graham to the very doorsteps of Reinhold Niebuhr. This leads to an interesting question. If *Reinhold Niebuhr* has not succeeded in stirring New York City for Christ, what chance has Billy Graham? The issue is not academic. It involves the very essence of Christianity.

Billy Graham defends Christian orthodoxy, while Reinhold Niebuhr defends Christian realism. Orthodoxy mediates problems of man and history from the perspective of Scripture, while realism mediates problems of Scripture from the perspective of man and history. This is the difference between these two positions, but how does this difference work itself out in practice?

Since Reinhold Niebuhr restricts himself to issues arising out of modern life, he enjoys a provisional advantage over Billy Graham. Realism subjects theology to very severe tests. Unless a doctrine answers to the religious and moral needs of twentieth-century man, it is cast into the fire and burned. This is one reason why young seminarians often find realism intellectually more stimulating than orthodoxy. Judged by the contemporaneity and dexterity of realism, orthodoxy seems unimaginative and vapid.

Reinhold Niebuhr's theological abilities were verified when he delivered the celebrated Gifford Lectures. The Lectures called for a critical interaction with issues that concern cultured people in an age of great anxiety. Reinhold Niebuhr rose to the occasion with acceptable skill. He succeeded in chal-

Part Two originally published in the May 13, 1957 issue of *Christianity Today*. Reprinted by permission.

lenging human pride on every level of life. His finished work *The Nature and Destiny of Man* is now the systematic theology of Christian realism.

It is this prophetic defiance of religious and moral complacency that keeps Reinhold Niebuhr in the forefront of theology. Orthodox theologians often become so devoted to hallowed forms that they shrink from participating in the modern Christian dialogue. They rarely succeed in relating Christianity to the peculiar difficulties rising out of contemporary life. Furthermore, orthodoxy's reliance on revelation tempts it to overlook, if not forthrightly defy, the relative insights of science and philosophy. This partly explains why orthodox scholarship is often a full generation behind the times. It also helps explain why the theological leadership has been caught up by Christian realism. While orthodoxy is distracted by such questions as whether there is any common ground between Calvinists and Arminians, or whether the church will be raptured before or after the tribulation, Reinhold Niebuhr is quietly constructing a systematic view of sin, mercy, and the total creative and destructive possibilities of man.

Since he is such an astute observer of human nature, Reinhold Niebuhr has developed a rather profound insight into the polar tension between law and grace. Orthodoxy usually supposes that the law of love is only a convenient summary of the Ten Commandments. Reinhold Niebuhr scores this as a capital theological error. He properly contends that Jesus Christ gave substance to ideal human nature by actuating the terms of love. Only love can comprehend the self-transcending limits of human nature. Reinhold Niebuhr's insight into the essence of love is so broad in scope and so exact in detail that the dialectic of law and grace impinges on every area of human experience. The total enterprise of man is simultaneously inspired and judged by the heights of love in Christ Jesus.

I cheerfully acknowledge a personal indebtedness to Reinhold Niebuhr. It was only as I studied Christian realism, long after I graduated from seminary, that I began to sense the power of pride and pretense in my life. Orthodoxy has an easy conscience about its own sins because it does not understand the connection between Christ's active obedience and the total creative and destructive possibilities of man.

But back to the problem of the New York Campaign. Since Billy Graham defends the traditions of orthodoxy, it would seem that his prospects of stirring Manhattan for Christ are not very good. But this need not necessarily be the case, and for a very convincing reason.

When the man on the street asks about the plan of salvation, he receives very little precise guidance from the theology of Reinhold Niebuhr. This, I assert, is the grand irony of Christian realism. Reinhold Niebuhr can prove that man is a sinner, but man already knows this. Reinhold Niebuhr can develop the dialectical relation between time and eternity, but this is beyond the tether of a dime store clerk or a hod carrier. When it comes to the acid test, therefore, realism is not very realistic after all. A concrete view of sin converts to an abstract view of salvation. And all of this is a direct fruit of realism's decision to mediate problems of Scripture from the perspective of man and history. For example, Reinhold Niebuhr does not speak about Christ's literal cross and resurrection at all. He speaks, at most, of the "symbols" of the cross and the resurrection. But of what value are these symbols to an anxious New York cabby?

Billy Graham has no fear of New York City. Like David of old, he confronts his Goliath in the name of the Lord God of Israel. His sermons are drawn from the clear teachings of Scripture. He deems human speculation as flax before the flame. When Billy Graham rises to speak, he patterns his words after those of the Apostle Paul. "For I delivered to you as of first importance what I also received, that Christ died for our sins in accordance with the scriptures, that he was buried, that he was raised on the third day in accordance with the scriptures, and that he appeared to Cephas, then to the twelve" (I Cor. 15:3-4, RSV).

Billy Graham may not succeed in relating the biblical message to the total life of modern man, but he does succeed in telling a sinner how to go to heaven. God made a covenant with Abraham, and the blessing of this covenant is Christ. "Now the promises were made to Abraham and to his offspring. It does not say, 'And to offsprings,' referring to many; but, referring to one, 'And to your offspring,' which is Christ" (Gal. 3:16, RSV). Since God found none with whom He could enjoy fellowship, He began a new race of righteous men through the resurrection of Christ. Christ invested human nature with perfection by living a sinless life. He offered up this perfection as a vicarious sacrifice. The cross of Christ makes it possible for a holy God to receive penitent sinners into fellowship. "It was to prove at the present time that he himself is righteous and that he justifies him who has faith in Jesus" (Rom. 3:26, RSV). Here, perhaps, is the clearest line of demarcation between orthodoxy and realism — and Billy Graham knows it. Orthodoxy teaches that Christ propitiated an offended judicial element in the character of God. Realism does not. Moreover, orthodoxy contends that this difference decides the gaining or losing of the Christian gospel.

If a student of theology wants to examine the complex relation between law, grace, and human freedom, he may find Christian realism more rewarding than Christian orthodoxy. After Billy Graham has reviewed the plan of salvation, he has very little to add. Billy Graham has not been to seminary. He has no criteria by which to measure the shades of better and worse in the complex systems that vie for the modern mind. And his weakness pretty well sums up the weakness of orthodoxy itself. Orthodoxy *tries* to relate Scripture to the more technical phases of science and philosophy, but its efforts are seldom very profound. Orthodoxy does not know enough about modern presuppositions to speak with authority. Publishers confront such a paucity of first-rate orthodox literature that they must fill out their lists by reprinting the works of older apologists and divines.

Let us bear one thing in mind, however. When we say that Billy Graham does nothing but make the plan of salvation clear, we intend to pay him a gratifying compliment. As one studies the book of Acts, one finds that the apostles devoted most of their energies to this same task of clarification. Thus, if orthodoxy is naive, so were the apostles. What *is* the work of an evangelist, if not to tell sinners how to be saved? Billy Graham preaches Christ in such clear and forceful language that even a bartender can find his way to the mercy seat. This is why the multitudes discover a power in Billy Graham that they miss in Reinhold Niebuhr. Billy Graham may know little about the inner technicalities of theology, but he does rest in the full and undoubted persuasion that Christ was delivered for our offenses and was raised for our justification. And this is the good news that repentant sinners are waiting to hear. The common man is weary of theories; he is hungry for the gospel; he craves a firm note of authority. And Billy Graham meets this need. He stands before the anxious multitudes and thunders, "Thus saith the Lord!"

Despite its anachronisms and inconsistencies, therefore, orthodoxy remains a stronghold of biblical Christianity. It puts first things first. It preaches that "without the shedding of blood there is no forgiveness of sins" (Hebrews 9:22, RSV). If the church fails to tell sinners how to be saved, of what final value is anything else that is said?

Realism's diagnosis of human sickness is profounder than that of orthodoxy. No one can safely question this. But it so happens that sick people are more anxious to get well than they are to learn how sick they are. And since this is the case, it may turn out that Manhattan's granite towers will offer little final resistance to the message of Billy Graham. There *are* no giants in the sight of God.

CHAPTER EIGHT

Reinhold Niebuhr's View of Scripture

To compose an essay on Reinhold Niebuhr's view of Scripture is far from easy, for the topic (to my knowledge) is nowhere an object of direct attention in the vast and stimulating Niebuhrian literature. The reason for this omission is the "nonexistential" character of the topic. The significance of this will be clarified in due time.

If one were to follow ideal lines in defining Niebuhr's attitude toward Scripture, he first would review the whole of Niebuhr's philosophy of religion. After this, he would find the precise relation between this restricted question and the larger system. Since so ambitious a project would not be practical in this compendious account, however, a substitute plan must be arranged.

In the absence of the larger procedure, the best alternative is to devise a guiding criterion. If such a standard can be found, we will have a norm by which to advance our particular problem.

In the interests of economy, I choose the following as a working criterion: *Religious thinkers will submit to the Bible only as they despair of learning the meaning of life without assistance from God.* Before this criterion can be either accepted or rejected, it must first be understood.

The norm sounds more complicated than it really is. It simply means that since sin is a personal rebellion against God, and since rebellion is an expression of human self-sufficiency, it follows that the natural man will not yield to the revealed Word of God until it interests him, and it will never interest him until he discovers profit in such a submission. Whenever God's voice is of neither interest

Originally published as Chapter IX in *Inspiration and Interpretation*, ed. John Walvoord (Grand Rapids, Eerdmans, 1957).

nor profit, man remains autonomous. Only as one *hungers* for Scripture will he conform to its teachings.

Let us illustrate this point, using humanism, orthodoxy, and Roman Catholicism as examples. Let us indicate in each case whether, and to what extent, there is dependence on the Bible.

Since consistent humanism believes it can solve all its problems by a more critical application of methods devised by man, it owns *no* instance of dependence on special revelation. This is one end of the scale. Orthodoxy lies at the other. Convinced that nothing can be known about the destiny of a rebellious society unless God reveals it, orthodoxy cheerfully yields itself to *every* teaching of Scripture. If humanism has no interest in special revelation, orthodoxy has every interest. Roman Catholicism is a case unto itself. Although it accepts biblical authority in the abstract, it materially submits only at those places where the interests of the church are advanced. It is the living church, not the written Word, that is the supreme court in all decisions.

With these preliminary observations behind us, let us apply our criterion to Niebuhr's system. *To what extent, if any, does Niebuhr cast himself on the authority of Scripture?* If we can find an answer to this question, our assignment will be finished.

I

Niebuhr's Rejection of Immanence

Humanism says that man either does have, or could have, all the clues needed to explain everything worth explaining. The philosophy behind this optimism is called *immanence*. Immanence is the confidence that history contains its own meaning. Man needs only time and patience to acquire all significant truth. The Logos of history dwells within history.

The alternative to immanence is the spiritual admission that we cannot solve the meaning of life until some extrahistorical source of knowledge and power is found — which, in our case, is the Bible. Using our illustrations again, we note the following: humanism is built on immanence; orthodoxy rejects it at all points where questions about an offended God's attitude toward man are involved; and Catholicism courts it wherever it buttresses the interest of the church.

Although it does not follow that the rejection of immanence

implies a submission to Scripture, it can be said that only as a man despairs of solving history's problems within history will he long for a Word that proceeds from heaven. This is why it is crucial to discover Niebuhr's stand on the question. If he accepts immanence, we may safely conclude that he rejects any serious dependence on the Bible, and our study is finished; while if he rejects it, we may assume that he at least is open to the possibility of biblical authority.

Niebuhr emphatically rejects all forms of consistent immanence. "Man in his strength and in his weakness is too ambiguous to understand himself, unless his rational analyses are rooted in a faith that he is comprehended from beyond the ambiguities of his own understanding."[1]

To assist in the explanation of this quotation, let us grasp what Niebuhr means by "freedom." Freedom refers to man's simultaneous potentialities for creativity and destruction. Wherever one enjoys transcendence above nature, he is free. This is why Niebuhr asserts that a *solution to the problems raised by human freedom cannot be found by an extension of human freedom.* Since man is already out of harmony with the law of life, it follows that freedom cannot be its own redeemer. Freedom spreads its evil on every new level of life. Let us delay naming this disease until we have first observed its symptoms.

Classical liberal theology cites science and universal education as proof that man's control over existence is as inevitable as the hardening of the muscles in the arm of the blacksmith. Niebuhr rejects this sanguine optimism because it overlooks the element of corruption in all expressions of freedom.

Science cannot solve our problems for at least two reasons. *First,* it is not equipped to recognize the difference between neutral, empirical data and the prejudiced affections of the scientist. "The usual basis for this hope is the belief that there is no essential difference between the stuff of history and the stuff of nature and therefore no real distinction between the application of the 'scientific method' to nature and to history."[2] But there happens to be a qualitative difference between bunsen burners and the self-love of a technician. *Second,* a failure to perceive this difference encourages the error that mankind's troubles stem from a poor use of science, rather than from the evil that inheres in the will of man. This blindness fosters the very pride

[1] *Faith and History* (New York, Scribner, 1949), p. 101.

[2] *Ibid.*, p. 82.

and self-sufficiency that cause history's sickness. "The rise of the natural sciences was at first merely a by-product of this sense of human self-reliance, for nature was regarded merely as the mirror of the greatness of man. But as science gradually contributed to man's actual mastery of natural forces it gave a new impetus of its own to the idea of human self-sufficiency."[3]

Next comes education. By lying nearer spiritual vitalities, education is more easily confused with values that only faith can safeguard. Whenever education is equated with virtue, man betrays himself into the error of thinking that his life is natively in harmony with the right. But there happens to be a conflict between the mind's perception of truth and the egoistic interests of a very stubborn will. Education may tell us what is true, but it cannot affectionately conform man to the truth. At this point secular science and education join in falsely presupposing that man's life is causally continuous with nature. "The reason mechanistic psychiatry and psychoanalysis run easily into a justification of license is because they labor under the illusion that the higher self (they would scorn that term) is able to put all internal forces in their proper place, if only it knows their previous history and actual direction."[4]

But why are science and education agents of self-interest? Answer: Man is a sinner. Sin is man's stubborn refusal to accept the limitations of human nature. "Sin is to be regarded as neither a necessity of man's nature nor yet as a pure caprice of his will. It proceeds rather from a defect of the will, for which reason it is not completely deliberate; but since it is the will in which the defect is found and the will presupposes freedom the defect cannot be attributed to a taint in man's nature."[5] Since man participates in both time and eternity, he is tempted to pretend securities and finalities that are neither secure nor final.

> The brutality with which a Pharisee of every age resists those who puncture his pretensions proves the uneasiness of his conscience. The insecurity of sin is always a double insecurity. It must seek to hide not only the original finiteness of perspective and relativity of value which it is the purpose of sin to hide, but also the dishonesty by which it has sought to obscure these. The fury with which oligarch,

[3] *Human Nature* (New York, Scribner, 1941), p. 66.
[4] *Does Civilization Need Religion?* (New York, Macmillan, 1927), p. 21.
[5] *Human Nature*, p. 242.

> dictators, priest-kings, ancient and modern, and ideological pretenders turn upon their critics and foes is clearly the fury of an uneasy conscience, though it must not be assumed that such a conscience is always fully conscious of itself.[6]

It now ought to be clear why Niebuhr rejects consistent immanence. To repeat: *a solution to the problems raised by human freedom cannot be found by an extension of human freedom.* "Where there is history at all there is freedom; and where there is freedom there is sin."[7] Every individual and collective pretension to finality illustrates man's contentious refusal to accept limitations that are native to creatureliness.

The desperation of our predicament can only be understood as one recognizes that sin soothes man into believing that evil in history is the fault of others, never his own. Any *personal* repentance before God is either superfluous or dangerous: superfluous because it suggests that man is not sufficient unto himself—while he is; and dangerous because it substitutes reliance on God for human industry. With stentorian boldness Niebuhr speaks against the complacency of modernity. He voices judgment against a decaying bourgeois-liberal culture; he indicts its pretensions and securities on every level of life.

Let us now return to our initial criterion: *Religious thinkers will submit their minds to the Bible only as they despair of learning the meaning of history without assistance from God.* Since Niebuhr rejects consistent immanence, we are safe in concluding that he at least is open to the *possibility* that the answer to life is found in Scripture. Whether this possibility eventuates in personal appropriation must now be investigated.

II
The Twilight Zone of Transition

Although both Barth and Niebuhr share the existential presuppositions of Søren Kierkegaard, Niebuhr refuses to follow the Barthian stress on the complete discontinuity of time and eternity. Man is depraved, but he is not so depraved that he is unaware of his depravity. If sin were to blot out man's memory of original righteousness, man could never be goaded into creativity by a feeling of his own moral shortcomings. Niebuhr, thus, affirms a clear point of contact between God and the secular world.

[6] *Ibid.*, p. 256.

[7] *Human Destiny* (New York, Scribner, 1943), p. 80.

In developing a philosophy of natural revelation, however, Niebuhr is careful to guard against immanence. A penumbra borders nature and grace. It may be identified with neither immanence nor transcendence. It is not in immanence, for it speaks against human self-sufficiency; and it is not in transcendence, for man is able to discover it apart from special revelation. Natural revelation points toward, but is not part of, special revelation.

The contents of natural revelation cannot be laid on the table for curious eyes to inspect. Before a person can be sensitive to the voice of God in his heart, he must learn to think *existentially*; that is, from within the sensitive center of his own inner responsibilities and conflicts, and not after the manner of objective speculation. An existential perspective is a concerned perspective — a concern for what it means to be a responsible, existing individual: to tremble when friendships and loyalties are betrayed, to fear when duties are neglected, to grieve when ideals are dethroned.

When Niebuhr finished analyzing the sickness of society, he concluded that harmony is destroyed because pride inflates each one to believe himself finally secure over against his neighbor. No other thesis can account for the piety with which men defend their own interests. Whether in driving a car down the street — where one is angry at another for inconsiderateness — or in a collision between national interests that leads to war, the same sinful disease of pride is at work. It soothes man with the comforting assurance that his interests are universally valid — taking care, of course, to conceal the radical disparity between pretense and conduct.

Evil in history can only be eliminated as individuals and nations substitute sympathy for belligerency and intolerance. But such spiritual modesty is not possible until one appreciates the distance that separates his own evil ways from the perfection of the "law of life." This, however, is an existential insight. If one refuses to view the problem from within his own evil life, he will never submit to God's righteousness. He will never perceive how greatly his devotion to duty is corrupted by personal interest and finite perspective. He will never realize that the law of perfection stands in opposition to, rather than in harmony with, the vitalities of his own ego. It is the strategy of pride to urge the ego to believe that a lovely harmony unites its own with universal duty.

Niebuhr is careful to show that the law by which we judge others, and hence the law by which God judges us, is *the law of love*. Tolerance, forgiveness, and pity are the basis of a just society. The law of love is the law of life.

Existential experience testifies that whenever an individual courageously tests his life by the law of love, he is confronted by two important facts. *First*, that the law of love stands in judgment upon the pretensions of the ego. Interests are sinful whenever they are entertained at the expense of the rightful securities of others. *Second*, that judgment comes from the person of God. Conscience is an outlet for eternity's dissatisfaction with the raw elements that nest in the bosom of the heart.

The more existentially one analyzes the elements in this moral confrontation, the more accurate will be his definition of the God who deflates pride. Man is able to know God in three complementary ways. "The first is the sense of reverence for a majesty and of dependence upon an ultimate source of being. The second is the sense of moral obligation laid upon one from beyond oneself and of moral unworthiness before a judge. The third, most problematic of the elements in religious experience, is the longing for forgiveness."[8]

But what is the significance of this discussion? What is the relation between natural revelation and Niebuhr's view of Scripture? Now that our findings have become complex, how shall our original criterion be applied? Two observations must be made.

First, having despaired of discovering the meaning of life apart from a rule of eternity that is discontinuous with tribal particularities, Niebuhr submits to whatever biblical insights support this need. The Bible authoritatively witnesses to the fact that God stands in judgment over all human pretensions. Jehovah is *never* an extension of personal interests. He is eternally wrathful against all claims to individual or tribal virtue. Human acceptance is by grace, not merit. No man is worthy to look on God. "Israel does not choose God. God chooses Israel; and this choice is regarded as an act of grace for which no reason can be given, other than God's own love (Deut. 7:7-8). In Biblical thought, the grace of God completes the structure of meaning, beyond the limits of rational intelligibility in the realm of history, just as divine creation is both the fulfillment and the negation of intelligibility for the whole temporal order."[9] Modernity's disease is a

[8] *Human Nature*, p. 131. If the reader has an opportunity to study Niebuhr's own arguments, let him check the entire context here. Niebuhr goes to great length to clinch his point.

[9] *Faith and History*, pp. 102-103.

result of its proud insistence that eternity is morally continuous with finite interests, a view that leaves the particularities of culture in perpetual war with each other. Finitude has no norm by which one partiality can be judged superior to another. It has no resources of forgiveness when hostilities end. The Bible is God's Word because it is not an extension of either individual, tribal, or national pride. God simultaneously judges and completes history.

Second, and more important for our study, there is a *dialectical* necessity for biblical revelation. Here is our predicament: if we *deny* the law of life, we court moral skepticism; but if we *admit* this law, we place both ourselves and society under a condemnation from which there is no earthly deliverance. We cannot keep the law of love; yet we corrupt our own dignity if we cease to try. This is the basis of a dialectical tension.

A "dialectical tension" is formed by contrary relations — as when two individuals take exception to each other's opinions. Their manner of speech is a dialogue; its purpose is to bare a truth that is acceptable to both parties. There are, in Hegelian terms, three parts to the dialectic: the thesis, the antithesis, and the synthesis. Thesis and antithesis are the contrarieties. The synthesis develops as contrarieties elicit latencies from each other. Niebuhr's theology rests on a formal acceptance of the principle that time and eternity are related dialectically, i.e. after the manner of a dialogue: time creates polar tensions which are resolved only as eternity speaks — a process which is never static and completed, but which is repeated at every moment within the spiritual life of the penitent.

Niebuhr's social theology is premised on the following dialectic. *Thesis*: nothing less than the law of love can define righteousness. *Antithesis*: neither the individual nor the collective mind meets the terms of this righteousness. These are the contrarieties of the dialectical tension. But this is the limit of the human perspective, for only *Christ* can elicit a synthesis.

Throughout the two volumes of the Gifford Lectures, Niebuhr persuasively argues that only biblical Christianity correctly comprehends and resolves the dialectic. The sweep of non-Christian, religio-philosophical literature betrays familiar, nondialectical conclusions: either the law of life is misunderstood and some furious, demonic vitality replaces the cohesions of fraternity — as in the Nazi ideology; or the law is understood, but its implications misunderstood — as in all forms of immanence.

> The fact that a culture which identifies God with some level of human consciousness, either rational or super-rational, or with some order of nature, invariably falsifies the human situation and fails to appreciate either the total stature of freedom in man or the complexity of the problem of evil in him, is the most telling negative proof for the Biblical faith. Man does not know himself truly except as he knows himself confronted by God. Only in that confrontation does he become aware of his full stature and freedom and of the evil in him. It is for this reason that Biblical faith is of such importance for the proper understanding of man, and why it is necessary to correct the interpretations of human nature which underestimate his stature, depreciate his physical existence and fail to deal realistically with the evil in human nature, in terms of Biblical faith.[10]

Only biblical Christianity is truly dialectical, for it alone announces the law with perfection, while yet judging all pretensions to fulfillment.

This is not to suggest that the biblical witness is *consistently* dialectical. Like other human writing (so Niebuhr argues) it is corrupted here and there by finite perspective and personal interest. But faith overcomes these inconsistencies and seizes the announcement of heaven that in the epoch of Christ's life and death a dialectical solution to the relation between God's justice and His mercy is defined — a solution the Old Testament prophets sought but could not find.[11]

III
Dialectic and the Authority of Scripture

Remembering the terms of our criterion (*that religious thinking will submit to the Bible only as they despair of learning the meaning of history without assistance from God*), we are now ready to sum up the relation between Niebuhr's dialectical theology and the authority of Scripture. Since he believes that nondialectical truths can be developed within immanence, Niebuhr interacts with Scripture only at those places where the Bible is dialectical. In order that we might understand how this takes place, let us set down a series of steps, using each as a point of departure for the next; this procedure to continue until our goal has been reached.

[10] *Human Nature*, p. 131.

[11] It is impossible to document these propositions within the short compass of this chapter. Those who are interested in pursuing the theological ramifications should read the primary sources.

First, Niebuhr breaks from the liberal doctrine that the Bible was developed within immanence. It is not a record of the religious experiences of men. "This historical revelation is by no means simply the history of man's quest for God or the record of man's increasingly adequate definitions of the person of God, interpretations to which modern liberal thought has sometimes reduced Biblical revelation."[12] Scripture *judges* the pretensions of immanence.

Second, the Bible is an account of the covenantal (dialectical) relations between God and Israel. It tells of the moral obligations upon the part of a responsible, responding people and the twofold, personal Word of God — mercy and grace when men walk humbly before Him, and judgment when they persist in sin. The Bible is "the record of those events in history in which faith discerns the self-disclosure of God."[13] God comes into history and reveals Himself through Israel.

Third, although the Bible is a record of how God deals with a covenant people, it is not a system of propositional truth that can be tested by the law of contradiction in the light of regenerate experience, as in orthodoxy. Its truth is perceived existentially-dialectically, not critically-historically. Scripture illuminates and interprets the confrontation faith experiences whenever the transcendent self meets God on the edge of history. "What it discerns are actions of God which clarify the confrontation of man by God in the realm of the personal and individual moral life. In personal life the moral experience consists of the moral obligation as being laid upon man not by himself, nor yet by his society but by God; as a judgment upon man for failing in his obligation; and finally as the need for reconciliation between man and God because of the estrangement resulting from man's rebellion against the divine will."[14]

Fourth, as an objective book, therefore, the Bible is marred by the same errors and inconsistencies that corrupt any human document. Niebuhr accepts destructive higher criticism as a legitimate tool when examining Scripture.

> Yet early Biblical history has many facets which relate it to lower particularistic religion. The canon of the faith contains an "Old Testament" in which we find the usual "story" of a particular people, seeking to comprehend their history in terms of their origin. Their God is the God of "Abraham, Isaac and Jacob," who seems to be,

[12] *Ibid.*, p. 136.
[13] *Ibid.*
[14] *Ibid.*, pp. 136-137.

> on some levels of their history, simply their champion against competitors and foes, both allowing and enjoining them to the most ruthless actions in order to encompass the defeat of the foe and to establish their own security.[15]
> The Deuteronomic code was an effort to place legalism in the service of prophetism and to give to prophetic insights the permanence of legal codes.[16]
> The suffering servant figure is not a Messianic symbol; or, if so, only in a very secondary sense. Most probably it was meant to designate the nation rather than any individual. If so, it represented a profound effort to give the sufferings of Israel a higher meaning by the suggestion that its mission and triumph in the world would not be achieved by the usual triumph over others but by the vicarious suffering for the sins of others.[17]

The truths of the Bible lie behind the time-bound forms in which they are expressed. They can only be "existentially" perceived.

Fifth, since transcendence has no more rights over immanence than immanence has over transcendence, it is illicit for Christians to use the Bible as an authority in fields that are accessible to the unaided intellect: science, history, philosophy, and the like. Unless faith succeeds in disengaging the accidental from the essential and the marginal from the central, it will fall into a literalism that converts the paradox of biblical Christianity into complete absurdity. Let us enlarge upon this matter.

Faith must separate nondialectical elements — genealogies, the dimensions of the temple, and the like — from those which are richly dialectical, though garbed in terms appropriate to immanence (biblical stories, such as creation and the fall of man). The latter are depth insights. Wherever they may be found, and under whatever conditions they may appear, depth insights are true. Take the fall of man, for example. When tested as history, it turns out to be an artless Hebrew narrative which betrays the prescientific mentality of an early mind; but when tested existentially, it mirrors profound truth. It accurately explains the transcendental experience of a morally sensitive individual. Although one may earnestly *assent* to the law of life, he nevertheless experiences a "fall" whenever he tries to conform his conduct to this

[15] *Faith and History*, p. 24.
[16] *Human Destiny*, p. 39.
[17] *Ibid.*, pp. 44-45.

perfection. The biblical account of Adam and Eve is "religiously," though not scientifically or historically, true. It is a "myth" of the Hebrew mind, a transcultural truth is stated in terms drawn from an earlier culture. Faith accepts the story as a "symbol" of its own experience. Sagas and myths represent the transcendental effort of both individuals and groups to "seek a deeper or higher dimension of meaning than the mere record of their continuance in time."[18] The Bible is rich with symbols: Babel, the Ark and the Temple, the Son of Man, the Cross, the Resurrection, the Second Coming, the Antichrist — symbols that lose their value the moment they are taken literally. Niebuhr believes that the literalizing of symbols is the capital error of orthodoxy.

Let us illustrate Niebuhr's philosophy of symbolism by the following rather meaty passage:

> The symbol of the second coming of Christ can neither be taken literally nor dismissed as unimportant. It participates in the general characteristic of the Biblical symbols, which deal with the relation of time and eternity, and seek to point to the ultimate from the standpoint of the conditioned. If the symbol is taken literally the dialectical conception of time and eternity is falsified and the ultimate vindication of God over history is reduced to a point in history. The consequence of this falsification is expressed in the hope of a millennial age. In such a millennial age, just as in a utopian one, history is supposedly fulfilled despite the persisting conditions of finiteness. On the other hand if the symbol is dismissed as unimportant, as merely a picturesque or primitive way of apprehending the relation of the historical to the eternal, the Biblical dialectic is obscured in another direction. All theologies which do not take these symbols seriously will be discovered upon close analysis not to take history seriously either. They presuppose an eternity which annuls rather than fulfills the historical process.[19]

Sixth, in summary: the Bible is the record of a redemption history (*Heilsgeschichte*) that completes life from a perspective beyond history. Redemptive history mirrors individual history by dialectically balancing the following triad: the eternal justice of God (law); the failure of man to abide by law (sin); and the grace and mercy of God in Christ (forgiveness). The biblical testimony about Christ is what a pious soul experiences in Christ. But if we confuse a

[18] *Faith and History*, p. 23.
[19] *Human Destiny*, p. 289.

"witness" to truth with a corpus of infallibly revealed propositions, we convert a profound understanding of Scripture into a distressing literalism.

> The Reformation insistence upon the authority of Scripture as against the authority of the church, bears within it the perils of a new idolatry. Its Biblicism became, in time, as dangerous to the freedom of the human mind in searching out causes and effects as the old religious authority. But rightly conceived Scriptural authority is meant merely to guard the truth of the gospel in which all truth is fulfilled and all corruptions of truth are negated. This authority is Scriptural in the sense that the Bible contains the history, and the culmination in Christ, of that *Heilsgeschichte* in which the whole human enterprise becomes fully conscious of its limits, of its transgressions of those limits, and of the divine answer to its problems. When the Bible becomes an authoritative compendium of social, economic, political and scientific knowledge it is used as a vehicle of the sinful sanctification of relative standards of knowledge and virtue which happen to be enshrined in a religious canon.[20]

Conclusion

Here is the sum of the matter: *Since he is pessimistic about the success of immanence, though not about man's ability to develop a dialectical philosophy, it follows that Niebuhr retains a critical autonomy over the system of Scripture.* Whether such autonomy is good or bad depends upon how seriously one accepts or rejects the Bible as a system of thought. Orthodoxy is persuaded that one has no final truth about God until he submits to the Bible's self-testimony. Neo-orthodoxy judges the Bible by dialectical insights; orthodoxy judges dialectical insights by the Bible.

Let us remember the *interests* that encourage Niebuhr to reinterpret the biblical system after the lines of myth and symbol. He does not come to Scripture to learn whether sin is so awful that Christ's atonement propitiates an offended element in the nature of God; not whether the rejection of this blood results in the judicial sentence of the sinner to hell; not whether God has so committed His will to writing that those who love Him prove their affection by a complete and unreserved submission to the whole counsel of Scripture. Rather, he has sought an answer to this one

[20] *Ibid.*, p. 152.

question: "Is it possible to join the existential experiences of man with a hopeful philosophy of both history and society?" Niebuhr feels that apart from biblical presuppositions, this simply cannot be done. Therefore, he defends the Bible as the Word of God.

CHAPTER NINE

Niebuhr's Criteria of Verification

I
Introduction

Realizing that bad subjectivity frequently travels under the name of good existentalism, Niebuhr cheerfully faces the problem of proof:

> How is one to judge the eternal word and to know when the prejudice of an hour or the foolish opinion of a man has been falsely arrayed in the pretense of divine wisdom? The history of religion is full of the chronicles of both fools and knaves and our insane asylums still boast their due quotas of unhappy maniacs who think they are messiahs. By what criterion is one to discover what is true and what is false in the conflicting claims of competing messiahs and prophets?[1]

But Niebuhr refuses to cast pearls. Since chair-fast pedants frequently use questions of verification to evade spiritual commitment — their clamant cries for proof serving as cloaking for an indurate soul — Niebuhr dissipates no energy on an arid academicism. He deliberately etches a portrait of reality, transcendently persuasive if examined soulfully within D. H. Lawrence's "terrifying honesty," but tenuous and unconvincing if the self ensconces to the narrow corridors of its empirical life, limiting meaning to laboratory operations and gauging both the self and others with depersonalized objectivity. Christian faith is apposite only as one existentially accepts his bistratal milieu: body

Reprinted by permission from *Reinhold Niebuhr: His Religious, Social and Political Thought*, ed. Charles W. Kegley and Robert W. Bretall (New York, Macmillan, 1956).

[1] *Beyond Tragedy*, p. 93.

and soul, time and eternity, involvement and freedom; recognizing that his claim to natural security is interlarded with pretentious spiritual arrogance. Niebuhr is too moved by reality's dialectical complexity and man's impartible wholeness to offer Christian paradoxes on the platter of simple rational persuasion, take it or leave it. Academic noncommittalism is but the lengthening shadow of a turgid ego. Men who are too secure in themselves find the gospel irrelevant, and foolish because irrelevant.

II
Pre-Soteric Proof

Convinced that too little commerce between nature and grace is dialectically as dissatisfying as too much, Niebuhr firmly disaffiliates himself from Kierkegaardian-Barthian discontinuity. Evidences for Christianity lie both "in" and "out" of grace. If the gospel invades our experience in the manner of a cast stone, without reason or defense, Christian claims hold no antecedent advantage over non-Christian.

> The final truth about life is always an absurdity but it cannot be an absolute absurdity. It is an absurdity insofar as it must transcend the "system" of meaning which the human mind always prematurely constructs with itself as the centre. But it cannot be a complete absurdity or it could not achieve any credence. In this sense Kierkegaard goes too far.[2]

Like other time-eternity issues to pass across Niebuhr's desk, "common ground" is resolved by a "yes" and "no" held in "fear and trembling." "The Truth contained in the Gospel is not found in human wisdom. Yet it may be found at the point where human wisdom and human goodness acknowledge their limits, and creative despair induces faith."[3] A penumbral zone of universal concrete reality borders revelation and culture, making minimal tests of competing religious claims possible and leaving all without excuse. An underprizing of man's native ability to assess, though not resolve, his moral predicament, inevitably corrupts the dialectic from the side of either nature or grace.

Affirmative pre-soteric proof swivels on the fixity of this one truth: namely, that human nature is tensionally mounted within an unconditioned obligation to fulfill the very moral law

[2] *The Nature and Destiny of Man*, II, 38n.
[3] *Ibid.*, p. 206.

that involvement is impotent to actuate. Only as man consciously incarnates selfless love is he integral; yet each new effort at fulfillment betrays the self into something less than selfhood. Hence the antecedent persuasiveness of Christianity: *It is the only world view that defends hope in man and meaning in history within an honest acknowledgment that the libido is spiritually informed with law-defying vitalities not subject to mind.* Niebuhr's argument is as neat as that. Whenever one admits (*a*) that love is the law of life and (*b*) that inordinate affections transmute each level of fulfillment into a more refined base for egoistic security, he must, if consistent, move on to Christianity. Niebuhr shows from individual and collective experience that man is inevitably, though not necessarily, a sinner, and that only biblical theism convincingly resolves the law-sin dialectic. Until this Herculean literary effort is appreciated, affirmative pre-soteric proof, like the cross itself, will remain foolish.

Ironically, this very honesty denudes prophetic insight of its power to persuade those who are too worldly wise to sense mind's role as a minion of vagrant impulse. When rationalists curtly dismiss the cross, they think they act solely on the authority of a pure-metal use of reason; though in reality they are somewhat guided by the counsels of powerful personal interest. Pride prefers peace in sin rather than through the forgiveness of sin.

Negative pre-soteric proof turns on this: *that every effort to define the end of history from some perspective within history ends in a threat to both life and history.* Again, a very neat piece of persuasion. Niebuhr gauges the superiority of dialectical to nondialectical insights by the degree that each defends (*a*) the intrinsic dignity of the individual and (*b*) a collective order wherein personal creativity and social justice enjoy fullest outlet. Nothing can preponderate these values, whether prophet's voice, confessional standards, or ecclesiastical tradition. "The final test of any religion must be its ability to prompt ethical action upon the basis of regard for personality."[4]

This is the pith of the matter: If the distinctiveness of dialectical religion consists in the *exclusion* of any level on which freedom may enjoy an easy conscience, nondialectical distinctiveness consists in its *inclusion*. In the stead of God who judges and forgives sinners from a perspective beyond history, some absolutized aspect of either form or vitality serves as a rallying point for the faithful on the one side, and a guide in eliminating nonconformists on the other. This results in either a premature flight from history or a procrusteanizing of creativity to

[4] *Does Civilization Need Religion?* p. 31.

fit some individual or tribal virtue. The one leads to other-worldliness, the other to this-worldliness — equally noxious, though not equally cynical, eventualities.

Other-worldliness abandons history's possibilities to a manageable "second best" in which a regnant caste of zealots or conceited philosopher-kings manacles the social order to personal interests: overlords who identify perfect social orderliness with the peaceful preservation of the *status quo*, as in Plato's pathetic stratification of life in the *Republic*, or the outraging of human dignity in Brahmanic and Buddhistic acosmic pantheism. "A human righteousness, which is not subjected to a purer righteousness than anything to be found in nature or history, must inevitably degenerate into a fanatic self-righteousness."[5] *This-worldliness* inflates hegemonic powers to exempt themselves and their cause from divine judgment by excluding some favorite virtue from the general ambiguity of history. Roman Catholicism sanctifies static feudal injustices on the confidence that, as "the continued incarnation of Jesus Christ," she is vested with perpetual divine authority over all human institutions. Protestantism recoils from medievalism, only to sanction dynamic injustices in a laissez-faire physiocracy that separates the proletariat from the ties of soil and fealty that held the feudal community together. Despotism replaces the milder claims of holy men with bold pretensions of racial homogeneity or utopianized versions of society; baiting its toadies with ridiculous promises and brutalizing malcontents with an iron fist. In brief: *nondialectical ideologies inevitably defend some "party line" in which truth is selfishly tied in with the interests of the privileged* — an outraging of life's dignity at its core.

III

Soteric Proof

Evidences "in grace" form no *arcanum*, accessible only to initiates and whispered among votaries in spiritual jargon, for Christianity fulfills rather than negates the general experience of the race. *Yes*: man is able to perceive the things of the Spirit, for he is made in the image of God; *no*: man is not able to perceive the things of the Spirit, for sin has corrupted the image. The one side safeguards responsibility and the other the universal need of the cross. From this insight Niebuhr develops a dialecticized version of the relation between nature and grace: *Christian revelation preserves, even as false religions inevitably corrupt, the values of individual dignity and social justice that*

[5] *Beyond Tragedy*, p. 242.

all men natively seek. Proof "in grace" thus consists of no more than a cataloging of evidences to buttress this Christian claim. Whether such data are convincing will depend entirely on the degree to which an individual first understands and appreciates (*a*) his own longing for dignity and justice and (*b*) the tragic way that nondialectical alternatives mismanage them. The Christian case is as follows:

Individual dignity: First, *the vicious circle of self-love is interrupted*. The self expires whenever it tries too desperately to rescue itself from within itself:

> But the self lacks the faith and trust to subject itself to God. It seeks to establish itself independently. It seeks to find its life and thereby loses it. For the self which it asserts is less than the true self. It is the self in all the contingent and arbitrary factors of its immediate situation. By asserting these contingent and arbitrary factors of an immediate situation, the self loses its true self. It increases its insecurity because it gives its immediate necessities a consideration which they do not deserve and which they cannot have without disturbing the harmony of creation. By giving life a false centre, the self then destroys the real possibilities for itself and others. Hence the relation of injustice to pride and the vicious circle of injustice, increasing as it does the insecurity which pride was intended to overcome.[6]

The cross teaches men to save their life by losing it. Individuals neutralize anxiety's decaying effects by casting themselves on the mercy and love of God who sublimates man's fragmentary existence within the security of the divine perspective. Second, *the sting of the law is removed*. Humility before God issues in the inner satisfaction that a just relationship maintains between God's judicial demands and the moral predicament of the sinner. Although conscience continues to remind man of his distance from life's norm, it is powerless to destroy confidence that life has meaning beyond this vale of tears:

> The good news of the gospel is that God takes the sinfulness of man into Himself; and overcomes in His own heart what cannot be overcome in human life, since human life remains within the vicious circle of sinful self-glorification on every level of moral advance.[7]

Third, *evil is explained without dividing man against himself or history against its norm*. The Greeks glorify mind and undervalue body, unmindful that too much confidence in mind is itself part of man's evil. Kant unmasks the maxim-defying ten-

[6] *The Nature and Destiny of Man*, I, 252.
[7] *Ibid.*, I, 142.

dencies of radical evil, but he despairs of integrating this insight into the wider questions of the Critique. Idealism resolves the problem by winking at both the unity of will and the anchorage of mind in sub-rational impulse. Nietzsche canonizes man's robust capacity for self-deception by transmuting the "hidden lie" into the "honest lie."

> All of these beliefs are pathetic alternatives to the Christian faith. They all come finally to the same thing. They do not believe that man remains a tragic creaturé who needs the divine mercy as much at the end as at the beginning of his moral endeavors. They believe rather that there is some fairly easy way out of the human situation of "self-alienation."[8]

Without Christian insight into the height of man's freedom and the depth of his sin it is impossible to diagnose the true cause of history's sickness, for sin consistently places evil outside the self. Fourth, *universal history is established.* Since the temporal process is such a checkerwork of comforting regularity and distressing impertinence, historians either formulate a truncated philosophy from partial perspectives, or they despair altogether at finding unified meaning.

> There are, in short, tangents of moral meaning in history; but there are no clear or exact patterns. The moral obscurities of history must either tempt men to the despairing conclusion that there is no meaning in the total historical enterprise and that history is merely a bewildering confusion of "death for the right cause, death for the wrong cause, paeans of victory and groans of defeat," or that it is under a sovereignty too mysterious to conform fully to the patterns of meaning which human beings are able to construct.[9]

Christian faith comes to history's moral ambiguity by way of judgment and forgiveness. Whenever a man turns from history's contradictions long enough to deal seriously with the contradictions in his own heart, he is introduced to a God wise enough to have a plan that transcends all rational systems devised within history.

A working social order: First, *an effective tie between persons is named.* Perfect justice is defended by a loving respect for the individual. Nuances of inequity can be detected only as the obligation of life to life flows from the infinite task of sacrificial love. "Love is thus the end term of any system of morals. It is the moral requirement in which all schemes of justice are fulfilled

[8]*Christianity and Power Politics,* p. 7. "The way of the wicked is like deep darkness; they do not know over what they stumble" (Proverbs 4:19).

[9]*Faith and History,* p. 132.

and negated."[10] When less than the intimacy of the whole person is accepted and defended, injustice becomes both natural and inevitable, with no checks against powermongers who make certain that others, never themselves, suffer the injustice. Second, *an effective motive in social action is named.* Love is easy when consanguinity and mutual interest prevail, but how shall it sustain its sweetness before an incorrigible, obdurate selfishness? If love must justify itself within the temporal process, it is engulfed with disappointment; but if love is abandoned, the norm of world brotherhood yields to the tyrannizing of life within calculated interests. Niebuhr rightly grounds the motive of love in Jesus Christ:

> We are to forgive because God forgives (Matt. 18:23); we are to love our enemies because God is impartial in his love. The points of reference are vertical and not horizontal. Neither natural impulses nor social consequences are taken into consideration.[11]

This insight, in turn, relieves the inner distresses that ensue whenever the self is consciously committed to futilitarian ends. Satisfaction with the right, while provisionally vindicated by love's rewards, is finally supported by filial pleasure toward God.

> The paradox of religion is that it serves the world best when it maintains its high disdain for the world's values. Its social usefulness is dependent upon its ability to maintain devotion to absolute moral and spiritual values without too much concern for their practical, even for their social usefulness.[12]

A working political order: First, *the collective ego is set under a principle of self-criticism.* Power is an "evil necessity"—necessary because of man's stubborn defense of interests, yet evil because it is an extension of partiality at the expense of perfect brotherhood.

> Perfect power and goodness can be united only in God, where the contest of life with life is transcended and where the possession of power does not lead to its misuse in the struggle for existence. In human history disinterested power is never as disinterested as it claims to be. It always insinuates something of the special interests of a participant in the struggle of life into the pretended position of disinterested preservation of justice.[13]

[10] *The Nature and Destiny of Man*, I, 295.
[11] *An Interpretation of Christian Ethics*, p. 46.
[12] *Does Civilization Need Religion?* p. 77.
[13] *Discerning the Signs of the Times*, pp. 140-141.

When force is not held as a sacred trust from God, wielders of power, whether autocratic or mobocratic, quickly fall prey to pride's counsel that *their* particular employment of power is a virtuous extension of divine right. "Man is always most inhuman, not when he is unconsciously driven by natural impulse, but when he imagines his natural impulses and his relative values to be the instruments of some absolute good."[14] Second, *perfect political ends are harmoniously joined to realistic means.* Marx shrewdly understands (*a*) that interests growing out of the division between "mine" and "thine" create history's sickness, and (*b*) that towering ideologies are consciously or unconsciously a partial rationalization of these interests. But his sagacity ends with the perversion that both the worker and his defenders are as innocent in their person as they are pure in their doctrine; and that proletarian resentments, not being part of the natural order, are deciduous affections that wither away with the complete socialization of property. "This is one reason, and perhaps the chief reason, why the communist alternative to the injustices of our civilization has universally created greater injustices and hatched more terrible tyrannies than previously known in history."[15] The only way to check this or any other political conceit is by a prophetic-dialectical religion that places the pretenses of the collective ego within the general ambiguity of history. Only biblical insights can defend equality without creating a new caste of heavenly surrogates that confuse the perfection of the ideal with the perfection of their person. Democracy thus is relatively better than other political schemes, and that for three definite reasons:

> The first is that it assumes a source of authority from the standpoint of which the individual may defy the authorities of this world .... The second is an appreciation of the unique worth of the individual which makes it wrong to fit him into any political program as a mere instrument .... The third insight is the biblical insistence that the same radical freedom which makes man creative also makes him potentially destructive and dangerous, that the dignity of man and the misery of man therefore have the same root.[16]

A basis for tolerance: Here is the paradox of knowledge: Christian truth is final because it accepts the existential intimacy between interest and idea; yet part of this finality is its consistent

[14] *Reflections on the End of an Era*, p. 171.
[15] *The Irony of American History*, p. 165.
[16] *Christian Realism and Political Problems*, p. 101.

denial that individuals may have final truth. Christian insight is not scepticism, yet it is. It is confidence "in faith," yet despair "in fact." Renaissance optimism embraces the scepticism, but rejects the faith, only to end by losing an integral element in tolerance.

> To meet the test it is necessary not merely to maintain a tolerant attitude towards those who hold beliefs other than our own. The test is twofold and includes both the ability to hold vital convictions which lead to action; and also the capacity to preserve the spirit of forgiveness towards those who offend us by holding to convictions which seem untrue to us.[17]

Scepticism issues in a provisional kindliness toward dissenters, but it is impotent to evaluate the fine shades of better and worse in life. The luxury of scepticism easily converts to the noxiousness of irresponsibility; which, in turn, makes the masses prey to a clever autocrat who tools his own finalities within either pragmatic expediency or tribal interest. Only Christian faith can cradle final truth within the humble denial that final truth can be had.

IV
Critique

Niebuhr cannot be evaluated with clinical objectivity. The most that one can do is to place oneself in the middle of the warmth and challenge of the system, sensitively matching Niebuhr's claims with the witness of reality itself. Critical estimates cannot be decisive; hence, a compromise that the reader must patiently accept.

I find the pre-soteric criteria entirely compelling. The more I ponder Niebuhr's arguments, the less successful is my escape from their force. But the soteric standards seem somewhat less than satisfying. Try as I may, in my most charitable moments of meditation, I am unable to avoid concluding that Niebuhr's theology rests on disappointing subjectivism and scepticism.

Subjectivism: Niebuhr eloquently assures us that "the suffering of God is . . . the voluntary acceptance by divine love of the consequence of sin,"[18] but how is this claim proved? An examination of the fine print reveals that final authority for filial peace in God rests not on Christ or the apostolate but — surprisingly —

[17] *The Nature and Destiny of Man*, II, 219.

[18] *Ibid.*, II, 56.

on the subjective feeling of the penitent. "Whenever the power of sinful self-love is taken seriously there is a concomitant sense of gratitude in the experience of release from the self. It is felt that this is a miracle which the self could not have accomplished."[19] But does this really end the matter? That the penitent may sense an inner peace which structurally resembles forgiveness, I do not question; but has Niebuhr given the *only* possible interpretation of this serenity? Psychology of religion abundantly witnesses to the inner deceptions of which the human psyche is capable, especially when it is borne away in the partial madness of religious ecstasy. May not "peace of heart" actually represent an extension of self-sufficiency on a higher and more mysterious plane? Niebuhr is confident that inner manifestations of sin can be named, thus assuring an individual that his assuaged conscience represents a work of God and not the fruit of mystic, psychotherapeutic forces in the man himself. An appeal to the "experience of the race" strengthens Niebuhr's case verbally, though not factually, for if one individual can confuse strands of inner complacency with divine forgiveness, many can persist in the same error. Niebuhr cannot appeal to objective authority without conceding that the relation between time and eternity is not exclusively dialectical; yet apart from such an appeal, so it seems to me, a Luther can only answer an Eck by pointing to inner feelings that Eck would immediately equate with some extension of egoism. Hitler, we are informed, nursed a steady confidence that he was under the special protection of God. If so wretched a heart as his could be soothed, of what deceptions is the penitent capable, whose very posture of humility convinces the ego that the first step toward safety has been taken? Niebuhr's appeal to the Bible gives the impression of being lifted from the quagmire of subjectivism, and for this happy inconsistency I register thanks; but in such a case he solves the dialectical riddle by plowing with my heifer.

Scepticism: Insights of both Marx and depth psychology persuade Niebuhr that reason is too immersed in the vitalities and interests of life to be an innocent source of final truth. Name the conviction; it is conditioned by peculiar circumstances, "*as all convictions are*."[20] "All human knowledge is tainted with an 'ideological' taint. It pretends to be more true than it is. It is finite knowledge, gained from a particular perspective; but it pre-

[19] *Ibid.*, II, 115. "The sinner must feel himself 'justified,' that is, he must feel that his imperfections are understood and sympathetically appreciated as well as challenged." *Reflections on the End of an Era*, p. 285.

[20] *Moral Man and Immoral Society* (1947 edition), p. 166. Italics mine.

tends to be final and ultimate knowledge."[21] This seems clear enough. Yet one is quite perplexed at the nonchalant way in which Niebuhr himself claims final truth. "The revelation of the Atonement is precisely a 'final' word because it discloses a transcendent divine mercy which represents the 'freedom' of God in quintessential terms: namely, God's freedom over His own law."[22] Niebuhr's main "finalities" include Christ, the cross, the law of love, Renaissance optimism, and Reformation pessimism. The reason that Niebuhr needs finalities is far more obvious to me than the justification of his simultaneous denial of and claim to final truth. Indeed, if the obligation to be tolerant is not final, it cannot consistently be argued that intolerance is normatively wrong for tomorrow; but how does Niebuhr prove its finality?

Closer inspection shows that when Niebuhr speaks of Christian insights as "final," he means to extend the claim only to a "knowledge of the limits of knowledge," a knowledge, in short, that suffers from no context, being directed toward the ground of being.[23] I am unpersuaded by this distinction. A "knowledge of the limits of knowledge" is hardly as rich as the assertion, "We must be tolerant because God, in Christ, has first been tolerant of us." The one is formal, the other factual. By drawing on such ontologic references as God's existence, nature, and will, Christian convictions are anchored in material truth. Whether or not Christ died for sins is partly a matter of historico-critical research. The transcendental significance of the cross proceeds *through* these objective, contextual facts. It seems, despite all, that Niebuhr's defense of tolerance rests on the same scepticism that underlies bourgeois secularism.

I am not haggling over theological centesimals; I speak to questions that spell the gaining or losing of the Christian world view. Either tolerance rests on the scepticism that final truth cannot be had, and thus Christianity's objectivity is lost; or we widen our epistemology to include final, contextual knowledge of God, Christ, sin, grace, and forgiveness, and then the relation between time and eternity is no longer exclusively dialectical. Either the dialectic renders final truth invalid, or final truth renders the dialectic invalid. This is a forced option.

[21] *The Nature and Destiny of Man*, I, 194.
[22] *Ibid.*, II, 67.
[23] Cf. *ibid.*, II, 217-218, Note 4.

CHAPTER TEN

Reflections on Aspects of a Christian Ethic

Part One
A Christian Social Ethic

Social ethics deals with the question of just relations between members of a group. When an individual is treated justly, he experiences a sense of dignity and well-being; when he is treated unjustly, he does not. Thus the white man's shameful dealings with the Negro can serve as a fertile field of investigation for the student of social ethics.

This may be well and good, but how does it affect the Christian worker? Should not such a worker devote himself exclusively to the cause of the gospel?

These questions cannot be answered until an important distinction is drawn. Apart from the light cast by such a distinction we may confuse the duties of the *church* with the duties of an *individual member* of the church. Every church member, whether or not he is ordained to preach the gospel, must associate with other human beings, and to the degree of this association he is part of a social order. Such membership carries responsibility.

The duties of the church include the preaching and defense of the gospel, the comforting and edifying of believers and the providing of help for the needy. The substance of these duties is in no way altered by the kind of society of which the church happens to be a part.

The duties of an individual member of the church include wholehearted support of everything that falls within the cause of the gospel and wholehearted support of everything that falls within the cause of justice. Whenever a believer downgrades justice he offends the whole counsel of God. "Thus says the Lord God . . . Put away violence and oppression, and execute justice and righteousness . . . " (Ezek. 45:9). The interests of the gospel and the interests of justice are not barbed incompatibles; they are gentle moral correlatives. If it is disturbing to see liberals neglect the gospel in their attempt to promote justice, it is no less disturbing to see conservatives neglect justice in their attempt to promote the gospel. The one should be done, and the other not left undone.

Conservatives should remember that God is righteous in His very essence. The atonement of Jesus Christ was heaven's answer to the just requirements of the law (cf. Rom. 3:25-26; 8:14, etc.). Hence the more we honor just relations, the more we bear witness to the divine image in us. Justice is a child of love, and love is the queen of the Christian virtues.

Conservatives must also be careful not to define saving faith too narrowly. Whenever we fitly believe on the name of Jesus Christ, we surrender every part of our life to the will of the Lord. Nothing is exempted from this majestic relationship. "We destroy arguments and every proud obstacle to the knowledge of God, and take every thought captive to obey Christ" (II Cor. 10:5).

Since the lordship of Christ permeates the initial act of saving faith, the pursuit of justice ought to be as natural as the founding of missions or Sunday schools. It so happens that a truly workable social ethic is structured on the disclosures and graces of the gospel itself. The highest criteria of righteousness flow from the very person of Christ. As William Cunningham wrote in *Christianity and Social Questions*:

> No mere humanitarian sentiment of brotherhood can compare with devotion to the living Christ, either in the range or the effectiveness of the appeal. It is the claim of Christ's gospel that it offers the most effective means the world has ever seen for influencing men personally and individually, by upholding an ideal for all to admire and to desire to imitate, an ideal which is so high that none can attain to it perfectly, and that yet lies so near that all may aim at it in every action of life.

Concern for justice is a clear sign that the love of Christ is actively at work within the heart of a believer, and it is by the cords of love that lost souls are drawn to consider the claims of the gospel. If a believer deliberately hinders the cause of justice, he may so outrage the lost that crucial opportunities to present the gospel will be surrendered.

Therefore, whenever a believer is afforded an opportunity to advance the cause of justice, let him seize this opportunity with all his might. But let him never be deceived into thinking that a citizen's crusade for justice will result in such pleasant utopian conditions that society can dispense with the church's preaching of the gospel. The regeneration of the social order — if we may use such language — awaits the blessed return of our Lord and Saviour Jesus Christ.

Part Two
Capital Punishment and the Bible

Although the question of capital punishment poses many difficulties, a Christian can be certain about a few things. In Romans 13, where the Apostle Paul develops the relation between church and state, the civil magistrate is given clear title to the use of the sword: "He does not bear the sword in vain" (v. 4). The sword refers to the power of life and death; it is "borne as the symbol of the magistrate's right to inflict capital punishment" (Vincent, *Word Studies in the New Testament*).

Nor is this all. The Apostle Paul says that the evil magistrate "is the servant of God to execute his wrath on the wrongdoer" (*ibid.*). This teaching directly opposes the oft-defended idea that the end of civil penalty is merely the reformation of the offender. Says Calvin, "This is a remarkable passage for the purpose of proving the right of the sword; for if the Lord, by arming the magistrate, has also committed to him the use of the sword, whenever he visits the guilty with death, by executing God's vengeance, he obeys his commands. Contend then do they with God who think it unlawful to shed the blood of wicked men."

Many critics of capital punishment — generally pacifists — rest their appeal on Jesus' command that we should turn the cheek, love our enemies, and never resist evil. But this appeal is irrelevant, for Jesus is speaking about *personal*, not *official*, conduct. The civil magistrate, let us remember, is an officer. Moreover, if the taking of life were intrinsically wrong, we would have to abolish the police force, the F.B.I. and all other law-enforcement agencies that rely on the power of the sword for the just execution of their duties. This would spell the end of a decent society.

Part Two originally published in the June 1961 issue of *Eternity*. Reprinted by permission.

Other critics of capital punishment argue that the taking of life is vindictive rather than remedial, retaliatory rather than preventive. But they argue from an assumption that attacks the very essence of civil law. Civil law is instituted for two purposes: to issue prohibitions and to punish transgressors. For example, it is unlawful to strike a federal officer or to contribute to the delinquency of a minor. Whoever commits one of these acts is liable to punishment. The same would apply to crimes that justly incur the death sentence.

Justice, let us remember, is the first concern of law. All other concerns are subordinate and derivative. We should do all we can to make our penal institutions humane; we should see that ex-convicts are welcomed back into society. But humanitarian efforts must respect justice. Otherwise we undermine existing judicial procedures. A civil-law society maintains elaborate court systems for one reason: to acquit the innocent and to punish the guilty.

A Christian should have little difficulty grasping this, for his own salvation rests upon a public act of legal punishment. Christ did not die merely to set a moral example. He died to propitiate divine justice. "It was the will of the Lord to bruise him" (Isa. 53:10). "This was to show God's righteousness, because in his divine forebearance he had passed over former sins; it was to prove at the present time that he himself is righteous and that he justifies him who has faith in Jesus" (Rom. 3:25-26).

But *when* should capital punishment be administered? There is really only one way in which a consistent Christian can answer this question. Capital punishment should be administered whenever justice requires it.

But this is not quite the end of the matter. As Christians we must join a responsible citizenry in applying the principle of justice to problems that plague lawmakers and bewilder jurors. And high among such questions is whether premeditated first-degree murder should automatically carry the death sentence.

Many Christians would say that the answer is self-evident. They merely cite Genesis 9:6: "Whoever sheds the blood of man, by man shall his blood be shed; for God made man in his own image." Since this precept dates from early biblical times, it appears to be a "creation" ordinance which is binding on all ages. The Mosaic law refined this precept of distinguishing between accidental and premeditated killing. Cities of refuge were provided for those who accidentally slew a neighbor. (See Deuteronomy 19:1-13, for example.) Since deliberate murder always carried the death penalty, it would seem that the Old Testament bequeaths an immutable principle of justice: a life for a life.

But the question cannot be settled quite so easily, for careful examination shows that the Old Testament did not follow a consistent approach to capital punishment — at least not when we judge by modern standards. A son was put to death if he cursed his father or mother (Exod. 20:17); but if a man struck and killed his slave, male or female, he was merely punished (v. 20). If a man lay with a beast, he was put to death (Exod. 22:19); but if he raped a virgin, he either married the girl or paid a sum of money (vv. 16-17). Examples of this kind could be multiplied. Where, then, is the immutable principle, a life for a life?

Such inconsistencies have convinced many Christians that the only permanent judicial elements in the Old Testament are the Ten Commandments and the rules concerning love and social justice. These elements are permanent, while the life-for-life precept is not, because the New Testament ratifies them. It would follow, on this position, that there is no specific biblical evidence to prove that premeditated first-degree murder must automatically carry the death penalty.

But this debate about the permanent elements in the Old Testament does not alter the fact that most Christians, down deep in their hearts, believe that calculated, cold-blooded murder calls for the death penalty. Hence, the spirit of Genesis 9:6 triumphs, despite all.

In any case, Christians would slight a clearly revealed teaching if they crusaded for a total abolition of capital punishment, for God has authorized the civil magistrate to use the sword against evildoers. Even common sense tells us that certain crimes must be severely dealt with: treason in time of war, conspiracy to kill an officer of the law, multiple murder, or a crime against humanity.

As for multiple murder or a crime against society, the very heinousness of such transgressions stirs up a sense of judicial horror which can only be appeased by capital punishment. For example, take the case of Harvey Glatman who attacked, photographed, and then strangled three young women in Southern California. When Glatman was convicted, the court said, "There are some crimes so revolting that the only proper punishment is the death penalty." Replied Glatman, "I think my actions justify that. I knew this is the way it would be."

Christians should not be deceived by secular arguments that fail to respect the relationship between civil penalty and justice. It is asserted, for example, that capital punishment does not deter others from committing murder. This assertion, if true, is beside the point. The point is justice, not deterrence. We do not imprison a car thief to deter others—at least this is not the *primary* purpose. The primary purpose is justice. Deterrence is a derivative element in civil law.

Other objections to capital punishment are equally beside the point, though for quite a different reason. Abolitionists often point to the fact (a) that wealthy people are rarely executed, (b) that minority groups are discriminated against, (c) that clemency is shown toward women, especially pretty ones, and (d) that justice at times miscarries and innocent persons are executed. These are serious points, but they do not specifically touch the question of capital punishment. Rather, they point to the residue of unavoidable tragedy that attends our present judicial system. Wealthy people can hire expert counsel to defend themselves against *any* charge; and juries will be vulnerable to prejudice regardless of what crime is being tried.

It is a grim fact, and no amount of Christian hand-wringing will change a line of it, that lawyers are often more anxious to win a case than they are to promote justice. Moreover, jurors are seldom convinced that civil penalties symbolize the divine wrath against evildoers. Jurors become emotionally involved with the accused, and soon they forget the seriousness of the crime and the demands of justice.

Although most objections to capital punishment are beside the point, there is one that is not, for it rests on a practice that flagrantly disregards the very principle of justice itself. Here is the problem: since modern society is saturated with assumptions drawn from humanism and the Enlightenment, some juries will resort to almost any expedient, rather than render a verdict that calls for capital punishment. This is a serious procedural flaw, and a Christian must come to terms with it. Were a Christian to *insist* that premeditated first-degree murder automatically carry the death penalty, he might obstruct the cause of justice.

What stand, then, should a Christian take? The answer is, he should take a stand for justice. He can help see that existing judicial procedures are made more realistic. Since we expect jurors to base their deliberations on delicate degrees of guilt in the defendant, it would only seem fair that the law should provide a wider range of penalties for specific crimes. For example, if conspiracy to commit murder carried either the death penalty or a life sentence without possibility of parole, jurors might find it easier to appease their conscience, and thus to follow through with a guilty verdict. A life sentence without possibility of parole would serve the cause of justice much better than the release of a defendant whose guilt is apparent but who is acquitted by a jury that shrinks from rendering a verdict that calls for capital punishment.

If our judicial system is to operate efficiently, we must see that justice is swift and sure. Old Testament justice meant something for this very reason. Unless charges of guilt can be established beyond all doubt, they should be dismissed forthrightly. But once guilt is established, the claims of justice should be met with dispatch. When a convicted man is given life in prison for conspiracy to commit murder, only to be paroled in a few years, we make a mockery out of our judicial system.

It may be necessary to review the whole question of capital punishment. But let the review be made in the name of justice, not sentiment. Atrocious crimes still call for the death penalty. A majority of Christians would agree with this, and so would a majority of U. S. law-enforcement officers. "It is my opinion," commented J. Edgar Hoover, "that when no shadow of a doubt remains relative to the guilt of the defendant, the public interest demands capital punishment be invoked where the law so provides."

Part Three

Should a Christian Go to War?

There is no more satisfying pleasure on earth than that sweet moral release from the penalty of sin which attends faith in Jesus Christ and a sincere renunciation of the things of this world.

This gift of regeneration consists in the crucifixion of our sinful nature and the implanting of new and holy affections. A Christian is a new creation; he is born again; he is one who, in the classic words of Thomas Chalmers, has had his love for the world driven out by the "expulsive power of a new affection." "O how love I thy law!" is the testimony of the regenerated heart. "How sweet are thy words unto my taste! yea, sweeter than honey to my mouth!"

And what is this code which defines the perfect law of obedience? Christ has expressed it: "The first is, 'Hear, O Israel: The Lord our God, the Lord is one; and you shall love the Lord your God with all your heart, and with all your soul, and with all your mind, and with all your strength.' The second is this, 'You shall love your neighbor as yourself' " (Mark 12:29-31).

Part Three published originally in the April 1951 issue of *His*. Reprinted by permission.

This statement is received by the Christian heart as the perfect law of life because it alone is able to measure the infinite shades of pride and egotism which form the very stuff of sinfulness. Sin is a preference of oneself to others. It issues in hatred and disrespect among men and defiance of righteousness before God. Pride and egotism are the parents of every friction. They breed lively offspring every season: "For men will be lovers of self, lovers of money, proud, arrogant, abusive, disobedient to their parents, ungrateful, unholy, inhuman, implacable, slanderers, profligates, fierce, haters of good, treacherous, reckless, swollen with conceit, lovers of pleasure rather than lovers of God, holding the form of religion but denying the power of it" (II Tim. 3:2-5). Every sin of the catalog can be traced directly back to pride and selfishness.

It is from such a life of sin that the Christian has been delivered.

While he may not live according to the exact law of love that he professes, he nevertheless leaps to his feet to testify that, being through with his old ways of selfishness, he now longs to imitate the life of sacrifice his Lord has set out for him. To return to a love of self and the world after tasting the sweetness of moral obedience in Jesus Christ is, in the words of Peter, to play the sow in the mire or the dog returning to its vomit.

It is a shocking experience for young Christians to realize that they live in such a complex social situation that the application of the law of love is exceedingly difficult, if not impossible. And worse than that, the Christian seems forced to submit to duties that appear but a carry-over of the old practices. And by all odds the most obvious, the most exasperating social order to which the Christian must adjust his new life is war. Armed conflict between nations appears the logical conclusion to the strategy of sinfulness: a bitter, bloody struggle for power which employs enormous expenditures of both men and material for petty ends, a strategy from which the Christian must disaffiliate himself unhesitatingly, always, entirely.

Are not the marching orders of the Christian clear? "You have heard that it was said, 'An eye for an eye and a tooth for a tooth.' But I say unto you, Do not resist one who is evil. But if any one strikes you on the right cheek, turn to him the other also; and if any one would sue you and take your coat, let him have your cloak as well; and if any one forces you to go one mile, go with him two miles. Give to him who begs from you, and do not refuse him who would borrow from you" (Matt. 5:38-42). Is it conceivable that a Christian is being obedient to these words when he joins a military force? May a Christian thrust a bayonet through the heart of a man and yet retain that sweetness and peace of heart which is the possession of those who, in obedience to God, make the law of humility and love their meat?

And yet, the instant the Christian imagines the consequences of not resisting evil forces with military might, he is staggered at the implications. For example: If the vicious intentions of the Politburo are not challenged by the armed might of the free nations, the obvious consequence upon the democratic world in general and the Christian community in particular would be enslavement of the citizenry, destruction of those freedoms which make worship possible, ravishing of our women and children, and easy slaughter or incarceration of those who fail to measure up to the trivial whims of the conqueror. And not only that: The more the ambition of the godless remains unchecked, the more the pride of the overlord will be inflated and the reach of his ambitions extended — until in the end, unopposed by any social mind on the face of the globe, the dictator will fain imagine that he is God and that the universe turns at his behest. The Christian recoils at this thought. He knows that the God of heaven and earth is a jealous God who will not permit sinful men to sit in His place of regal splendor and sport the holy crown which belongs to Him alone.

Then what is the solution? To whom shall the Christian turn? On the one hand the believer is commanded by Christ that under no circumstances is he to resist the evil person, while on the other he has the clear moral witness in his heart which assures him of the disastrous consequences that result when free people do not resist evildoers — consequences that, if permitted to ensue, would bring down shame and scorn upon the Christian religion itself. To permit a world dictator to swallow up the free people at his will is as unappealing to the sensitive heart as allowing a murderer to run loose in our large cities, riddling our children with a machine gun. What is the solution?

As the Christian matures in both faith and thinking, he learns that the Scriptures point out that there is a complexity within the social order. Recognition of this complexity will warn the one who is upset with this problem of war that in his enthusiasm to follow Christ he may have fallen into the error of reading into one aspect of life the directions that were intended for another.

The Scriptures teach that there are three independent spheres in life of which the Christian is simultaneously a member.

First, there is the home. In His covenantal dealings — in both Old and New Testaments — God addresses whole families, the promises being not only to the parents but also to their children. The father is the federal or responsible head of the home. This sphere is denominated in modern parlance as, "Your home is your castle." Neither church nor state can intrude in family matters.

Second, there is the church. The church in the wilderness centered around the tabernacle, while the church universal in the New Testament centers around the local congregation which is mystically united to all other believers through the body of Jesus Christ. Family distinctions are lost in the church, as we are all spiritually one in the Lord. In addition, the church may not be invaded by a government that sets its ritual, orders its doctrine, or prescribes the dispersal of its funds.

Finally, there is the state. Government is divinely ordained, as both Paul and Peter teach, for the purpose of praising the good and punishing the evil. "For rulers are not a terror to good conduct, but to bad" (Rom. 13:3). Man never decides that he ought to have government. Government is absolutely necessary as long as sin lasts, for sin turns men from the rule of God to selfishness; and this makes it necessary for law, regulation, and threats of order to proceed from the mind of the government. Without government there would be anarchy, a state of chaos in which every man does that which is right in his own eyes.

And the recognition of the biblical doctrine of the spheres helps in the solution of the problem of war. As long as there is woolly-mindedness on the matter of spheres, there will be a resulting confusion in ethics. The two always accompany each other.

One of the hardest things for young Christians to understand is the fact that family and church spheres are governed by an ethical standard which the civil body is not, and cannot be, governed by. The very suggestion of this fact is doubtless a stumbling block to those who, with an oversimplified view of Scripture and society, recognize neither the spheres nor the attending complexity of ethical requirements. It seems fantastic to such minds that any law except the law of love could be a divinely ordained medium of ethical obligation, for is not the whole gospel one sweet repetition: love, love, love?

There is no quarrel concerning the law that binds family and church, for all personal relations are expressed in love: the love of a family member for all the others and the love of a Christian for all within the body of Christ.

But by what standard is the government ruled? One must not say that the larger ego is bound by the same standards as the person, lest he be led into foolish and regrettable implications. The government is impersonal, a fact that must be written large over this discussion. The obvious reason for impersonality in government is that the larger ego lacks the very organs of sensitivity required for love. Love is a moral vitality which has no meaning outside of personality, for it involves the leaping of spirit into spirit with overtures of sacrifice and humility; and the result of love is an inner closeness which is spiritually satisfying.

A government is a thing, a relation, a center of power, a collective ego, an "Uncle Sam," an arm of strength, a rallying center for the interests and vitalities of a people. How then can it employ organs of personality to give and receive expressions of love? The government is established to protect interest, not to make self-sacrifice efficient. If men naturally sacrificed there would be no need for government; God would be King.

Since the larger ego of government is one step removed from the smaller ego of individual personality, it follows that the ethical code that defines its obligations is likewise one step removed from the ethic of love. The government is "the servant of God to execute his wrath on the wrong-doer" (Rom. 13:4). There is one, and only one, indubitable justification for government, and that is to bear the sword as an agent of God in the forceful restraining of wrongdoers. If all men consistently followed the law of love, there would be no need for government. But because men corrupt their freedom, seeking their own security at the expense of a neighbor's, it is necessary that government be on hand to keep the peace. Anarchy would prevail the instant the larger ego removed itself from the social scene.

The obvious reason why government cannot be obliged by the law of love is, thus, that God has created rulers only for this negative task of keeping the peace. The government is not the church. Government neither seeks out opportunities to be self-sacrificial in its own dealings, nor does it pass laws demanding that the citizenry live selflessly. The established rulers bother no man who never transgresses the rights of others and who promptly pays his taxes. This means that there is only one ethic that the larger ego respects: justice. Justice is a negative statement of the law of love; it is that ethic which forbids a person to transgress the rights of others. We are not to dump ashes in our neighbor's yard or send our bulldog against his children; we are to respect his rights. In summary: Government has been ordained of God, not to defend the law of love, but rather to execute vengeance against those who destroy existing forms of justice in society. When a ruler acts justly, nothing more can be required of him in his office. He is a good ruler.

It is popular for evangelists and evangelical ministers to teach that because we are citizens only of heaven and are merely passing through this world, the less we have to do with this filthy earth the better. Properly understood, of course, there is meaning here, for our ultimate interests are in Christ, not this world. But the danger of the formula is that it promotes that unhealthy civic quietism which blinds the Christian to his divinely ordained obligations as a citizen of the world he is passing through. "Let every person be subject to the governing authorities. For there is no authority except from God, and those that exist have been instituted by God. Therefore he who resists the authorities resists what God has appointed, and those who resist will incur judgment" (Rom. 13:1-2). Whether he likes it or not, the Christian is under solemn command from God to respond as a good citizen to the obligations placed upon him by the ruling authorities. He is to be obedient to the government in all ways except those which involve a transgression of the law of God; in which case he must serve God rather than man, just as did the apostles. But as long as the government is honestly seeking justice in the world, the Christian must be a faithful citizen.

This means that the Christian at times must perform the complex task of living according to two standards of life. In all matters pertaining to personal fellowship, he is governed by a sensitive obedience to the law of love; but when acting in an official capacity for the ruling ego, being armed with power to represent this impersonal mind, he stands under orders to discharge the rule of justice. For example: the police officer who is whisked to the scene of a robbery must, if he is a Christian, exhibit the law of love in all personal relations, while at the same time executing the law of justice as he acts in the official capacity of the arm of the law. As the fleeing youth is shot, therefore, the officer weeps in his heart, thus expressing the law of fellowship in his personal relations; at the same time he sternly executes justice as the one to whom power has been committed for keeping civic peace. Likewise, a judge in the courts must have no malice in his heart as he hands down severe decrees of judgment. As a man, he pities; as judge, he condemns.

If one will clear his mind and recognize the full implications of Scripture, he will see that this observation contains the solution to the problem of war, a solution based on this double standard of ethics, the one a measure of personal relations and the other, of impersonal. In areas of fellowship the Christian is never to resist an evil person or hold malice in his heart; while as one officially delegated by the state to execute the decree of judgment against those who refuse to stay within the bounds of justice, he trips the lever that opens the bomb door effecting the instant death of a hundred thousand people. If he personally hates those whom he is killing, he is no longer a good citizen of heaven, for God requires love from the heart under every conceivable situation; and if he refuses to do the killing when the government has decided the unrighteousness has reached that place where it can be stopped only through such armed resistance, then he is no longer a good citizen of this earth, for the first mark of a good soldier is obedience to his commanding officer.

When a soldier fights for justice in the armed forces, therefore, he is serving God, not man, for the government is divinely ordained to preserve justice by being a terror to evil ones. And how can government be a terror to wicked people except through force? When a murderer is on the loose, he cannot simply be handed a Gospel of John between crimes and then be left to himself to continue further killing. He must be resisted with force, for the wickedness in his heart operates on a different moral standard from that which love recognizes, fearing only the arm of law and order, not the frailty of either the family or the church.

Of course, it is needful that the government be on the side of righteousness before a Christian can conscientiously fight. And while it may be complex to determine when a government is the defender and not the aggressor — for motives are infinitely compounded with the subtleties of propaganda and emotion — *nevertheless the principle is incontestable that a Christian may not fight in either a preventive or an aggressive war.* The policeman may not shoot a boy he thinks is about to rob a bank. Law demands that the officer wait until the act has been committed before criminality is assigned.

Romans 12 and 13 join together these two facets of Christian living. Observe the exceptionless nature of the law of love: "Bless those who persecute you; bless and do not curse them. Rejoice with those who rejoice, weep with those who weep.... Repay no one evil for evil, but take thought for what is noble in the sight of all. If possible, so far as it depends on you, live peaceably with all. Beloved, never avenge yourselves, but leave it to the wrath of God" (12:14-19). Then observe the divinely ordained nature of government and the Christian's duty to obedience: "Let every person be subject to the governing authorities . . . . For rulers are not a terror to good conduct, but to bad. Would you have no fear of him who is in authority? Then do what is good, and you will receive his approval, for he is God's servant for your good. But if you do wrong, be afraid, for he does not bear the sword in vain; he is the servant of God to execute his wrath on the wrong-doer" (13:1-4). Paul runs these two expressions of the Christian life together without the slightest fear of contradiction. Man to man, one is always to love; nation to nation, the law of justice is the highest ethic that can reign.

The real heart of the problem of an active or passive relation to war is our view of man. The Scriptures teach that man, being born in sin, has an element of perversity in his nature which expresses itself in a lust for independence from authority. Sin is any resistance to the absolute authority of God, while evil is any resistance to the proper authority of either society, the church, or the home. The child expresses this perverse element early in life. It reflects a certain satisfaction when it turns aside from the clear directives in the home and stakes out in its own direction. Such perversity grows in efficiency as it becomes compounded with rational and technological fortifications, as seen in youthful delinquency, gangsterism in adulthood, and international plunder and conquest by nations.

There are two, and only two, ways in which this perversity can be met. The first are moral means. Grace is both common and special, common being all of the spiritual suasions in the heart short of salvation, such as dignities, fear of law, self-respect, etc.; special being the work of regeneration in the heart and the implanting of new affections. Second, there are the suasions of threats and force. These include the whole gamut of expedients which are resorted to in the three spheres. In the home there is the spanking; in the church there is discipline and excommunication; in the state there is the fine, the jail sentence, and execution.

Some make the law of love the sole standard in all spheres of life, denying the necessity of forceful means when coping with that overt perversity which has not been tranquilized by grace; but such people are blinded to the fact that the Scriptures do not teach, nor does life affirm, that evil will be overcome by the converting power of love. Love must reign in all personal relations; but wherever a perverse expression resists the moral overtures of love, civic or federal authority must apply sanctions proportionate to the resistance. A child must be spanked; the man guilty of incest must be excommunicated; the felon must be put in jail. In none of these instances may the law of love be broken in personal relations. The father loves the child whom he chastises; the church weeps for the erring; the judge grieves for the soul of the young man upon whom he must impose sentence.

Defensive warfare is simply the use of a national police force to destroy gangsterism on an international scale. The soldier is in exactly the same position as the civil officer at the scene of a bank robbery. Each must put down perversity with force. War is the last expedient to which a nation can turn when its survival is threatened by those who are bent on world domination and the lust for power. There is no doubt but that war is a terrible thing, almost too awful to speak of without tears in our voices. But the consequence of not matching force with force within the collective ego is infinitely less bearable. We will destroy the very securities within which men can preach and hear the Word of Life; we will betray all of the forms that guarantee our basic freedoms; and, worst of all, we will commit a sin against the very God who has ordained that Christian citizens be subject to those who have been placed in civil office as a praise to the good and a terror to the evil.

Part Four
The Secret of Loving Your Neighbor

In both the Old and New Testaments we are commanded to love our neighbor as ourself. This is a specific duty; its force cannot be evaded by sincere Christians. Our neighbor is anyone near us — a roommate, a passer-by, a fellow motorist, or any of the host of people who touch our lives during the day.

As Christians we tend to think that love is nothing but a set of right feelings toward our neighbor. But this only betrays the poverty of our understanding, for duty to our neighbor is grounded in an existing state of self-love. We must love our neighbor with the same degree of zeal and consistency with which we love ourselves. Self-love is the norm by which we measure the outgoing possibilities of charity toward a neighbor. This means that Christian love is a delicate blend of knowledge, feeling, and action.

Part Four originally published in the July 1961 issue of *Eternity*. Reprinted by permission.

The Golden Rule teaches us to do to others as we would that they should do to us. And what do we want others to do? We want them to treat us as human beings who are plagued with weakness, prejudice, temptation, dependent love needs, and a host of mysteries which escape precise detection and classification. And our neighbor is in the same predicament. He hungers for acceptance in the totality of his person. This is why we must do as we would be done by, for no other rule can take in man's self-giving powers as a creature made in the image of God.

Psychotherapy has proved that every normal individual craves love. The noted psychiatrist, Leon Saul, estimates that people crave love and care with an intensity ten times greater than they either know or will admit. And more than this, psychotherapy has proved that many of our adult anxieties trace to the persistence of feelings that are conditioned in childhood. Hence the persistence of mysteries in the personality. It has been well said, "Scratch an adult and you find a child." An insecure childhood is the seedbed of an insecure adulthood. Sometimes a child's craving for affection is either neglected or overindulged. Sometimes the harsh or unpredictable behavior of parents deprives a child of fixed standards by which to make a successful transition to the conforming pressures of modern society.

In any event, we are mysteries unto ourselves. We want to be better persons — more adequate, more able to accept rejection, less susceptible to resentment, less insecure — though we seldom become what we want. But our failure in no way relaxes either the self's love for the self or our craving to be approved by others. The mysteries are dear to the self because they belong to the self. The Lord says that we now must learn to do as we would be done by.

But since we tend to think more highly of ourselves than we ought, we lead self-centered lives. We become touchy and censorious. We revert to the manners of childhood by substituting competitive relationships for the adult responsibilities of sharing and serving. Children gratify their love needs by *getting*, adults by *giving*.

As long as we remain touchy and censorious, our neighbor will see nothing in our lives that will draw him to Christ. By failing to respect the dignity of our neighbor, we merely arouse his defense mechanism. He will be too busy defending his dignity to consider the claims of the gospel. When our attitudes are unblessed by love, our lives become empty and void (I Cor. 13:1-3). Uncharitable Christians alienate those who insist on being treated as *people* before they are addressed as *sinners*. Only new overtures of love can undo the damage caused by a want of love.

Since the Lord was filled with compassion, we can measure our own progress in sanctification by the degree to which we, in turn, are compassionate. For example, suppose we see a drunken man groping his way down the street. Our first impulse may be to use his sin as evidence that we are holy. But if we yield to this impulse, we only show how distant from holiness we actually are. We are guilty of trying to seem better by making the man seem worse.

We must denounce the sin of drunkenness, to be sure. But this obligation supplies neither cause nor occasion for a Christian to feel superior. We must love all men everywhere, even our enemies. And we prove the character of our love by sincerely doing as we would be done by. In the case of the drunkard we manifest Christian love by putting ourselves in his place. We then ask how we would want to be treated, were we bound by the chains of alcohol. Surely we would not want to be scoffed by high and mighty Christians. We would want to be understood and pitied. When a person drowns himself in alcohol, he is actually announcing that he is not able to cope with the fears and anxieties that imperil his life. He needs encouragement, not rejection.

Alcoholics Anonymous operates on a profound respect for the law of love, and not without reason. It knows that an alcoholic cannot get hold of himself, and thus come to terms with reality, until he is confronted with convincing spiritual assurances that others love and respect him. So a vital fellowship of concern is formed. A member of this fellowship will rise at any hour of the night to sit with a friend in need. Now, is it conceivable that Alcoholics Anonymous has risen to greater heights of compassion than the Christian church?

Followers of the Lord should not find compassion too difficult to come by, for we know that apart from the restraining influences of the Holy Spirit, we would all be prey to the very fears and anxieties that drive men to alcohol. All we have and are is a gift of divine grace.

Whenever our neighbor happens to be a Christian, we have a special reason to be kind and loving. In fact, some of the most beautiful passages in the New Testament are aimed at this duty. Sample: "Let all bitterness and wrath and anger and clamor and slander be put away from you, with all malice, and be kind to one another, tenderhearted, forgiving one another, as God in Christ forgave you" (Eph. 4:31, 32). Christians may engender hostilities in their very zeal to reach commonly accepted standards of perfection. They become so eager that they end up competing with each other. Moreover, the local Christian fellowship often converts to a cult which withdraws from fellowship with the church universal, and which devises its own status symbols and standards of hero worship. Cultic Christians reject believers in other traditions on the single charge that they do not wear the right denominational label. This, of course, is manifestly sinful.

Only richer works of love can deal with hostile, competitive relationships, and the base for this love is the love God has shown us in Christ. A mature Christian will remind himself that he is justified by faith. He does not have to be overly anxious about life, for he is already approved by the God of life. This tyranny of the self has been broken.

After a Christian learns to respect his neighbor as a human being, he then can create the kind of gentle rapport that will open the door for a scrutiny of those duties and values which lead to a richer concept of selfhood. But the Christian must first bear witness to the truth in his own life. If he is not kind and considerate, his overtures will be shorn of power. A genuinely mature Christian will show that it is possible for the self to save the self by losing the self, and he will show it to believers and unbelievers alike.

We are passing through a time of great social change, for a prophetic judgment is being leveled against tribal injustice, colonialism, caste privilege, racial discrimination, and denominational pretention in the church. The resulting disintegration of form can be ruinous for a person who is plagued by persisting childhood emotions, and who continues to imagine that he is a child in an adult world. He cannot cope with the feeling that he must stand mobilized against a hostile and changing social order. He desperately craves reassurance from those whose emotional maturity releases them to do as they would be done by. And who is better able to give this reassurance than Christians who know the meaning of divine forgiveness?

Anxiety and fear have such a grip on the social outlet that psychiatry has emerged as a powerful therapeutic agency. On every hand we see the pathetic effects of uprooted lives: alcoholism, divorce, delinquency, and a general relaxing of fixed moral standards. As Christians we can observe these facts with clinical detachment, of course. But shame on us if we do, for we have been called to share Christ's tears for a lost and dying world. We must serve as vessels through which the love of God can flow to needy souls. We must bear witness to a security that transcends the uncertainties and cruelties of a competitive society.

Our attitude toward men in general will be dictated by our attitude toward our neighbor in particular. Do we rise to the heights of the Royal Law by doing as we would be done by? Or do we use the faults of a neighbor as proof that we are superior? A choice must be made, though not a choice that can be made once and for all. It must be made each time we stand in the presence of another human being. It must be made every moment of *this* day in particular.

CHAPTER ELEVEN

The Virgin Birth of Christ

The Bible says that Christ was born of a virgin, but it does not say why. This silence has encouraged theologians to compose reasons of their own. These reasons, at times, are more ingenious than wise.

Some theologians say Christ's *deity* required the virgin birth, but the effort is wide of the mark. Christ is divine because He is one with the Father and the Spirit. The Trinity is an eternal order of being.

Other theologians say Christ's *incarnation* required the virgin birth, but the effort overlooks the sovereignty of God. Since God is omnipotent, He could have united divine and human nature in any way He elected. The mode of Christ's birth is part of the economy of redemption.

Many theologians say Christ's *sinlessness* required the virgin birth, but the effort is weak on several counts. First, a "traducian" theory of the soul is required; a theory, namely, that the soul of a child is not immediately created by God, but is derived from its parents by ordinary generation. Such a theory is pure speculation; the Bible nowhere tells how the soul is formed. Second, the apostles trace Christ's sinlessness to His holy life, not to His miraculous birth; and the judgment of the apostles is normative for the church. Third, the science of genetics has found that hereditary traits come from the mother as well as the father. Thus, the virgin birth would not, of itself, secure Christ's human nature from pollution.

Roman Catholicism tries to relieve the last difficulty by declaring Mary free from original sin. But the Roman expedient, taken out consistently, would imply a denial of the fall of man. Not only must Mary be immaculately conceived, but likewise her parents, her grandparents, and so on, until we reach Adam and Eve.

Originally published in the Dec. 7, 1959 issue of *Christianity Today*. Reprinted by permission.

Protestants say Mary *was* conceived in sin, and in saying so they void any causal connection between the sinlessness of Christ and the virgin birth. Just as God protected Christ's human nature from the pollution of Mary, so He could have protected it from the pollution of Joseph; in which case Christ would have been born of ordinary generation, yet without sin.

Theologians would be on much safer ground if they rested the case for the virgin birth on the manner in which God dealt with His covenant people in the Old Testament. Let us develop this.

When Adam sinned, he and all his seed incurred the just displeasure of God. Yet, grace triumphed over law in that very hour of woe. When all appeared lost, God said that the seed of the woman would bruise the head of the serpent (Gen. 3:15). The comfort of this prophecy was only surpassed by its mystery; for how could man, a willing servant of Satan, defeat the counsels of Satan?

God removed part of the mystery when he made a covenant with Abraham. God promised to bless all nations through the seed of Abraham. Abraham did not know how this would come to pass, but he believed God and it was reckoned to him as righteousness.

God removed more of the mystery when He instituted the Mosaic system of bloody sacrifice. The seed of Abraham would bless all nations by assuming the guilt of punishment into and upon himself. The Lamb of God, who takes away the sin of the world, was foreshadowed by the Mosaic system.

The Old Testament prophets concluded the economy of preparation by citing the name of the Saviour, the place and mode of His birth, and the manner of His life, death and resurrection. The Saviour would be born of a woman, and thus suffer the limitations of human nature. Yet, He would bear titles befitting His messianic office: Wonderful Counselor, Mighty God, Everlasting Father, Prince of Peace (Isa. 9:6).

Let us go one step farther. Since God's promises were greater than man's capacity to receive them, God always accompanied His promises with special signs. The spirit is willing, but the flesh is weak. For example, when Abraham inquired how he might know that God would bless him, God ratified the covenant by a smoking furnace and a flaming torch. When Moses feared Pharaoh's court, God gave him a rod of power. And when Gideon shrank before the Midianite hordes, God honored the fleece. These signs, in each case, were aimed at subduing the threat of involuntary unbelief.

When we see why God gave signs to His people, we can see

why Christ was born of a virgin; for if the great heroes of the faith required signs when they looked *forward* to the Saviour's coming, how much more were signs required by those into whose house the Saviour would be born? The signs of Christ's appearance had to admit of no doubt. Yet, the signs had to be secret lest the foes of righteousness begin their nefarious work before Christ's hour had come.

When the angel told Mary that God had chosen her to be the mother of the Saviour, she found the tidings awesome. "And Mary said to the angel, 'How can this be, since I have no husband?' " (Luke 1:34). The angel allayed Mary's fear by naming two specific signs: first, her own child would be conceived of the Holy Spirit; second, Elizabeth would bear a child in her old age.

In due time Mary was able to confirm both of these signs. When she felt life stirring in her body, she knew that her child was a miracle sent from God. And a happy visit to the home of Elizabeth confirmed the second sign.

As time passed, however, a new cloud of difficulty gathered; for when Joseph found that Mary was with child, he "resolved to divorce her quietly" (Matt. 1:19). Joseph's Hebrew piety, let alone his male ego, prompted this resolve. Not only had Mary brought shame on Israel by conceiving out of wedlock, but she had deliberately concealed her condition. This, at least, is how Joseph viewed the matter.

The cloud of difficulty did not lift until God dispatched an angel of light. "Joseph, son of David, do not fear to take Mary your wife, for that which is conceived in her is of the Holy Spirit; she will bear a son, and you shall call his name Jesus, for he will save his people from their sins" (Matt. 1:20-21). Convinced by this sign, Joseph took Mary to be his wife. Mary was now free to tell all that was on her heart. Mutual pardon was sought and forgiven. The holy couple then waited for God to give His gift to the world.

This pious vigil, however, did not end with the advent of Christ. The time of waiting, in fact, had hardly begun. Let us appreciate this as we ponder the virgin birth. Some thirty years elapsed between Christ's birth and His manifestation to Israel. During these years Joseph and Mary had no other proof of Christ's divinity than the signs surrounding His birth. Mary *prophesied* wonderful things about her Son, but she prophesied more than she understood. This is proved by the way she chided Jesus when He tarried at the age of twelve. "Son, why have you treated us so?" (Luke 2:48). Jesus replied to this query with divine authority, "How is it that you sought me? Did you not know I must be in my Father's house?" (2:49).

Few Christians are disturbed by the silence of the early church, for neither the book of Acts nor the Epistles make any explicit reference to the virgin birth of Christ. The difficulty, however, is easily resolved.

The mode of Christ's birth forms no part of the "one act of righteousness" by which Christ reconciled God to the world. When Christ died on the cross, He offered up the fruit of a perfected human nature. He earned this fruit by loving God with all His heart and His neighbor as Himself. Conscious, voluntary energy was required; an energy that Christ did not have as an infant, for His human faculties were undeveloped.

When the apostles preached the gospel, therefore, they had no more reason to refer to the mode of Christ's birth than they did to His legal parents or the street on which He lived. The gospel draws on the public ministry of Christ, a ministry that began with the baptism and ended with the resurrection.

The virgin birth is precious to the household of faith because it plays a major role in connecting the promises of the Old Testament with their fulfillment in the New Testament. "All this took place to fulfill what the Lord had spoken by the prophet: 'Behold, a virgin shall conceive and bear a son, and his name shall be called Emmanuel' " (Matt. 1:22-23 RSV). Scripture is inspired of God and has the force of law in the church.

During the joyous Christmas season, when we thank God for His inexpressible gift, let us renew our faith in the appointed means by which God made this gift to the world. God not only promised to bless all nations through the seed of Abraham, but He accompanied His promise with special signs. One of these signs was the virgin birth. If we disregard the virgin birth, we offend a confessional element that has united Christians from the first century until now.

CHAPTER TWELVE

Jesus Christ and Man's Condition

History raises questions to which Christ alone is the answer. The nations sense that man is not what he ought to be. Something is wrong; things could be better.

God's Image in Man

Man is anxious by reason of his distinctive capacities of moral freedom; and foremost among these capacities is that of self-giving love. Love is a sharing of natures. When man loves, God's power flows through him. "God is love, and he who abides in love abides in God, and God abides in him" (I John 4:16). Human personality is sacred because it mirrors the divine image.

Since man lives and moves and has his being in God (Acts 17:28), he enjoys a spiritual intuition of his own dignity from the first moment of moral self-consciousness. The evidence of this is near at hand. Whenever an individual is morally offended, the judicial sentiment is aroused within him. This sentiment stays aroused until the offending party either apologizes or repents, depending on the conditions. No individual is ever *taught* the fact of his own dignity. Self-love is the base from which everything else in life is judged.

The Confusion of Standards

Man's capacity to acknowledge God implies an equal capacity to deny God. Although Christ is the light of the world, He is not always received as such by those who lie in darkness. Celsus, for example, contended that Christ's ethic was commonplace. The exhortation to forgive enemies could be found in Plato, and more elegantly expressed at that. Gibbon made bold to say that the Golden Rule was formulated by Isocrates, four hundred years before the advent of Christ. And the Deists went on to argue that Christianity is as old as creation itself.

Published originally in the Winter 1960 issue of *Encounter*. Reprinted by permission.

When critics dismiss Christ on the charge that His ethic is formally similar to that of noble pagans, they confuse possession of truth with possession of virtue. If Christianity had nothing to offer but an ethical system, it would be as weak, and as subject to contradiction, as the systems of this world. Christianity is unique because its treasures are bound up with a Person. Christ requires nothing but what He first gives.

Paganism failed to see that *love,* not knowledge, is the true standard of virtue. Knowledge puffs up, but love edifies (I Cor. 8:1). Goodness is wanting unless a knowledge of the right converts to a performance of the right. "Love is patient and kind; love is not jealous or boastful; it is not arrogant or rude. Love does not insist on its own way; it is not irritable or resentful; it does not rejoice at wrong, but rejoices in the right" (I Cor. 13:4-6). Whoever is sensitive to the demands that he makes on others will perceive that he is already in possession of the law of life. Every normal child knows that a good person is one who is kind and thoughtful. Culture may condition the *manifestations* of virtue, but it does not account for the substance of virtue itself.

Original Sin

The natural man refuses Christ because pride cannot endure the scrutiny of divine judgment. "And this is the judgment, that the light has come into the world, and men loved darkness rather than light, because their deeds were evil" (John 3:19). Original sin awakens early in life, for it is characteristic of children to conscript the image of God into the service of pride. Children insist on being treated with fairness, but they are seldom willing to do as they would be done by. They try to appear better by making others appear worse. An adult may outgrow the blushing innocence of a child, but he continues to practice the child's habit of judging others by a standard that he neither does nor can live by.

Although fellowship with God is the highest good, man flees from God on the persuasion that he can complete his life by native resources. This declared autonomy arouses the judicial sentiment in God. "For the wrath of God is revealed from heaven against all ungodliness and wickedness of men who by their wickedness suppress the truth. For what can be known about God is plain to them, because God has shown it to them" (Rom. 1:18-19). Pride counsels man to overlook the derived nature of his own dignity. "There is no fear of God before their eyes" (Rom. 3:18). Man sets himself in the place of God; he loses himself by trying to save himself.

The Unconscious Prophecies of Heathendom

The classical Christian apologists were not disturbed by the syllabic affinity between the ethic of Christ and the ethic of classical paganism. These apologists knew that the distinguishing character of Christ is not information, but grace and truth. Paganism possesses valid information about God and virtue, but this does not empower man to love God or follow virtue. The more an individual tries to complete his life apart from grace, the more he confronts his own limits as a human being. The flesh and the spirit war against each other.

Xenophon was so sensitive to this inner conflict that he wondered if two souls lodged within him. Plato depicted human nature under the rich imagery of two winged horses and a charioteer. "The human charioteer drives his in a pair; and one of them is noble and of noble breed, and the other is ignoble and of ignoble breed; and the driving of them of necessity gives a great deal of trouble to him" (*Phaedrus* 246). Plato's language, at one point, is strikingly similar to that of James 4:1 : "Whence come wars, and fightings, and factions? whence but the body and the lusts of the body?" (*Phaedo* 66).

The woes of paganism are a prophetic witness to the limits and possibilities of unaided human nature. If a man refuses to be good, he corrupts his own dignity; but if he seriously throws himself into the work of virtue, he finds that his capacity for goodness is greater than his power to be good. "For the desires of the flesh are against the Spirit, and the desires of the Spirit are against the flesh; for these are opposed to each other, to prevent you from doing what you would" (Gal. 5:17).

This disparity between capacity and power prompted the classical philosophers to construct a "great chain of being" between God and man. From this metaphysical construction the philosophers deduced that human values were continuous with those of God, and that man may justly expect immortality in his nobler parts.

The classical poets went a step farther. They anticipated the incarnation of Christ by assuming that initiative in fellowship must come from God. Since man cannot ascend to God, God must descend to man. The poets are witness to the manner in which the world was ready for its deliverer. The decay of faith and the triumph of corruption were never so complete in heathendom but that the heart of man nurtured the hope that the gods had not forsaken their offspring. Thus, when Paul and Barnabas performed wonders in Lystra, they were called gods (Acts 14:11).

The classical poets are a rebuke to those Christian theologians who stress the corruption and depravity of man to the neglect of the image of God in man, which is man's truly distinguishing feature. Human nature is a fit receptacle for the divine being. Though Christ *humbled* Himself by taking on flesh, He did not *degrade* Himself.

The Foolishness of the Cross

The world was ready for its deliverer, but only on terms congenial with self-love. The world rejected Christ's righteousness out of an affected attempt to establish its own righteousness. Pride convinced man that the real man — man in his native self — is good. And man would stay good, were it not for extraneous influences. "For no man is voluntarily bad," observes Plato, "but the bad become bad by reason of an ill disposition of the body and bad education, things which are hateful to every man and happen against his will" (*Timaeus* 86).

Christ offended the Greek by denying that the rational man is the good man. Since the intellectual life is a willing servant of the vital life, man may be at his worst, not his best, when he is dedicated to the affairs of reason and mind. The intellectual life is no more virtuous than the vital life that informs it. Judgments appear more cogent when they are congenial with personal interest.

Christ offended the Jew by refusing to take sides against the Romans. An individual is not righteous because he is a son of Abraham. The Jews enjoyed custody of the oracles of God, but this custody was not, of itself, a justifying virtue. "Do not think that I shall accuse you to the Father; it is Moses who accuses you, on whom you set your hope" (John 5:45). Christ named the self-giving possibilities of love, not the pretenses of reason or race, as the true measure of virtue. By this measure all have sinned and come short of the glory of God. There is none righteous, no not one (Rom. 3:10).

The necessity of Christ's cross was dimly foreshadowed in the unconscious prophecies of heathendom, for in even the most cultured nations an elaborate theory of sacrifice had been worked out. The noble pagans sensed that the relation between God and man had been interrupted and disturbed. This relation could only be corrected by expiation.

An economy of sacrifice was never successfully woven into the classical philosophies, however, for the intellect cannot anticipate precisely what is implied by the idea of reconciliation between a holy God and sinful man. Man is man, not God.

Even Christ's disciples, with all their advantages, were offended when they learned that the Son of Man must suffer and die. The disciples knew that reconciliation would exact its price, but they never dared to conjecture that God would propitiate His own offended nature by offering up the Son on the cross. Apart from the light of Christ, the disciple could entertain no higher conception of reconciliation than that of the noble pagans.

Christ illuminates the world by revealing the manner in which God is pleased to receive many sons unto glory. Christ invested human nature with perfection by loving God with all His heart and His neighbor as Himself. This was His active obedience. On the cross He freely offered up this perfected human nature as a living sacrifice, thus propitiating the offended judicial sentiment in God. This was His passive obedience. By creating a new and holy race, Christ prepared the way for fellowship between God and man.

Justification by Faith

Since the stains of sin tincture every faculty in man, there is only one person who can stand in the presence of a holy God, and that is Jesus Christ, the God-man. Sinners must be clothed with the righteousness of Christ. This righteousness is received as a gift, through faith and repentance. "For no human being will be justified in his sight by works of the law since through the law comes knowledge of sin. But now the righteousness of God has been manifested apart from law . . . the righteousness of God through faith in Jesus Christ for all who believe. For there is no distinction; since all have sinned and fall short of the glory of God, they are justified by his grace as a gift, through the redemption which is in Christ Jesus, whom God put forward as an expiation [propitiation] by his blood, to be received by faith" (Rom. 3:20-25). Faith is the instrumental cause of justification.

Heathendom could only conceive an aristocratic salvation in which a few set themselves above their fellows. Justification was gained by a rational participation in the Logos of universal reason. The real man is the rational man, and man is at his best when he is thinking. No genuinely universal offer of salvation could be conceived because the measure of virtue was thought and not love. The intellectual elite were more moved by personal pride than by a compassion for the multitudes groveling in the mire of elementary passions.

Whenever man exempts some area of his life from the scrutiny of divine law, he is free to sanctify the most cynical fruits of pride. Plato, for example, believed that men are virtuous by their dialectical contact with the world of Ideas. He therefore stratified the Republic on the unconscious conceit that social privileges are determined by the extent to which a person succeeds in the discipline of dialectics. The result was a static communistic order in which the philosopher is king; the slave, a living possession. Plato could not free others because he could not free himself. Reason may soar to the world of Ideas, but contact with this world does not render a person either willing or able to be good. Man is not free until he is delivered from the tyranny of self-centered affections.

The worm of decay was at work during the very period when, to all outward appearance, paganism was in the full bloom of prosperity. Since man enjoys an intuition of his own spiritual dignity from the first moment of moral self-consciousness, in due season he will revolt against any social philosophy that blocks the normal channels of justice in the name of universal reason. "Great Nature's law, the law within the breast — Stamp'd by Heaven upon the unletter'd mind."

Christian Unity

On the eve of His suffering and death, Jesus prayed that His disciples would be so perfectly fettered by the bands of love that when the world saw the church, it would see the very unity of God: "that they may all be one; even as thou, Father, art in me, and I in thee, that they also may be in us, so that the world may believe that thou hast sent me" (John 17:21). There is only one way in which Christian unity can be enjoyed in history, and that is by a sincere and wholehearted submission to the law of life. "A new commandment I give to you, that you love one another; even as I have loved you, that you also love one another" (John 13:34-35). Christ says that we should have a sweet and kindly disposition toward all men, and especially toward those of the household of faith. Love mirrors the divine essence in a unique manner, for no man can genuinely love his brother unless the life of God flows through him.

Pride tempts Christians to substitute status symbols for the ties of love. Christians often think they have done their whole duty when they belong to the right church, or when they perform the right ceremonies or confess the right creed. The result is a spiritual smugness which substitutes cultic manners for the outreaching mission of the church universal. When the world sees the church, therefore, it often sees a knot of quarreling sects.

The early church was zealous to adorn the unity of the faith. "I appeal to you, brethren, by the name of our Lord Jesus Christ, that all of you agree and that there be no dissensions among you, but that you be united in the same mind and the same judgment" (I Cor. 1:10). Unity is a main characteristic of truth. When members of a family will not live together, they offend truth: the truth that love is the law of life, and that apart from love nothing else really matters.

Christians sometimes think that the church can be unified only by a specific theology or a particular tradition. In so thinking, however, they err, not knowing the Scriptures. Theology clarifies our view of the gospel, even as tradition unites us with our fathers in the faith; but neither theology nor tradition is the law of life. Love — and love alone — is the touchstone of true Christian unity. "Put on then, as God's chosen ones, holy and beloved, compassion, kindness, lowliness, meekness, and patience, forbearing one another and, if one has complaint against another, forgiving each other; as the Lord has forgiven you, so you also must forgive. And above all these put on love, which binds everything together in perfect harmony" (Col. 3:12-14). Love by-passes the accidents of life and reaches into the essence of the person. Love pities those who have not been taught a consistent theology; it succors those who do not participate in a classical church tradition.

When Christians use their advantages to frustrate the work of fellowship, they return to the ethos of heathendom. They hold the truth in unrighteousness; they forget that reconciliation is a gift of grace. "For who sees anything different in you? What have you that you did not receive? If then you received it, why do you boast as if it were not a gift?" (I Cor. 4:7). The final test of faith is fruit in the life, not profession with the lips. Does our faith tend, by a natural process, to render us more holy, more devout, more kindly, more charitable, more sober, and more humble? Does it make us more zealous for the peace and happiness of the church universal?

Christian Conversation

The willingness of Christians from different traditions to enter into serious conversation is one of the genuinely hopeful signs of the present hour. Conversation is more than a perfunctory means of acquainting others with what we believe, and why. It is a vital sharing of life; it is an authentic expression of Christian love. Conversation proves that we are incomplete without one another.

Happy the souls to Jesus joined,
And saved by grace alone;
Walking in all Thy ways, we find
Our heaven on earth begun.

Love sets Christ's kingdom apart from the kingdoms of this world. "Behold, how good and pleasant it is when brothers dwell in unity! It is like the precious oil upon the head, running down upon the beard.... It is like the dew of Hermon, which falls on the mountains of Zion! For there the Lord has commanded the blessing, life for evermore" (Ps. 133).

Christians who are willing to talk to each other may soon be willing to pray with each other. And in that blessed season of prayer, who knows what spiritual gifts God may shower in the church? "And all who believed were together and had all things in common; and they sold their possessions and goods and distributed them to all, as any had need. And day by day, attending the temple together and breaking bread in their homes, they partook of food with glad and generous hearts, praising God and having favor with all the people" (Acts 2:44-47).

CHAPTER THIRTEEN

Reflections on Contemporary Theology

Part One
On Karl Barth

Thanks to the ecumenical policies of Dean Jerald C. Brauer and the faculty of the University of Chicago divinity school, it was my privilege to serve on the panel of theologians who put questions to Karl Barth, on two evenings during the week in which he delivered in the university's Rockefeller Chapel a series of lectures entitled "An Introduction to Evangelical Theology." I shall never forget the experience. Professor Barth not only exhibited a scholar's control over the data of theology but radiated irresistible charm as a person. I congratulate Dean Brauer for persisting in the hope that he would some day succeed in bringing to America the colossus from Basel. I am a changed person as a result of Dean Brauer's persistence: changed in manners, convictions, and general pedagogy.

I do not wish to imply, however, that my dialogue with Professor Barth left nothing wanting. First, the questions that I submitted to him were in one sense not answered at all. Second, I was disturbed by the ease with which he employed the language of paradox. When I inquired, for example, about the metaphysical status of the devil, Barth was satisfied to speak of him as "an impossible possibility." Perhaps I need another course in logic, for the language of paradox strikes me as plain "weasel-wording."

Let me illustrate. Suppose my wife, on returning from a weekend trip, were to ask if I had fed and clothed the children according to our agreement, and suppose I were to reply, in a mood of detachment, "It is an impossible possibility." I am sure that my wife would look me in the eye and demand that I answer with a plain Yes or No. To violate the law of contradiction, whether in marriage or in theology, is no innocent matter.

In Chicago I had to sit tall whenever Barth decided to use his Christology as a norm by which to judge the relevance of other portions of Scripture. I realize, of course, that every theologian must be guided by some kind of hermeneutics. But in Barth's case I wondered if his particular hermeneutics does not tend to lead him away from the whole counsel of God as revealed in the Bible. Barth forthrightly claims to be a "theologian of the Word." But would it not be more accurate to say that he is a theologian of *part* of the Word — that part which is congenial with his Christology?

My doubt is summed up in a question I had planned to put to Barth but could not for lack of time: "Since you tend to reconstruct theology from the viewpoint of Christology, are you not obliged to disparage the dualism which has characterized historical evangelicalism — namely, that the faithful, covenant-keeping God dealt with faithless, covenant-breaking man under not one, but two federal heads, Adam and Christ?" (For biblical evidence of this dualism, see Rom. 5:12-21. Here the Apostle Paul develops the relation between Adam and Christ in systematic, didactic language. In my opinion this passage must be taken seriously by all who claim to be evangelical.)

I presume — though I may err — that Barth's prejudice against natural theology is traceable to the period in which he studied under Harnack and company at the University of Berlin. In due season Barth recoiled from liberalism's tendency to strip the gospel of special grace. And it was only a short step from this recoil to the supposition that natural theology is a demonic discipline which seduces believers into trusting the wisdom of the world rather than the Word of God. If Christ is our sole avenue to God — as Barth never wearies of insisting — then it would seem that the validity of natural theology is disqualified *ex hypothesi*. Little wonder that Barth has never found it easy to appreciate the works of Emil Brunner.

Barth's position against natural theology should be taken with a grain of salt, however, for in his *Church Dogmatics* he uses arguments that are drawn from natural theology. Perhaps the most glaring example is found in II, 3, pages 297-299, where he refers to the music of Mozart as "clear and convincing proof that it is a slander on creation to charge it with a share in chaos because it includes a Yes and No, as though oriented to God on the one side and nothingness on the other." Observe that Barth does not hesitate to use the word "proof" when pressing the achievements of Mozart into apologetic service.

Reference to Mozart provides us with a transition to what I consider the most critical question: Barth is unctuous in his praise of the music of Mozart, even as he is of the grace and wisdom of Christ; but does he in either case succeed in doing more than giving vent to his own feelings? I think not.

While collecting my thoughts for this article, I listened to *The Marriage of Figaro* — there should be no doubt about my regard for Mozart. But if my house were to catch fire I feel certain that I would rescue my recording of Gounod's *Faust* in preference to any of my Mozart recordings. Such a gesture, however, would in no way establish Gounod's superiority as a composer, nor would any praise of Gounod on my part make significant critical difference one way or the other.

In a similar way it seems to me that Barth advances the cause of truth not at all when he speaks of Mozart as the "incomparable" one, and of his music as the very "food and drink" of a Christian. He is only telling us something about his feelings and preferences, just as he would in declaring that he considers a pipe a greater delight than a cigar.

In his lectures at the University of Chicago Barth claimed to speak in the name of a community that had been confronted by God in Christ. And he fortified this claim with power and eloquence. In fact, he preached to us. But it takes more than power and eloquence, more than the assertion that we are contemporary with Scripture, to deliver our theology from the hovering threat of subjectivism. The moment we downgrade the historical and logical elements in biblical revelation — preferring instead to stress the element of personal confrontation — we are in the subjective area of feeling. Sympathetic emotion may be interesting, but it should not be confused with objective truth.

What is to prevent the most radical cultist from resorting to his own brand of "feeling" theology? In such a case, the theology of the cultist might, were he an able preacher, rank as high on the ladder of truth as that defended by Karl Barth. I realize that what I am saying would not disturb Barth. During the first of the two discussion sessions I asked, "How would you deal with a person who claimed to be confronted by God while listening to the music of Mozart and leafing through a telephone book?" I was trying to suggest that "feeling" theology could get alone quite well without the Bible. But, so far as I could tell, Barth saw neither relevance nor force in my question. I dropped the issue, though my conviction remained unchanged.

From the above it should be obvious that I suffered some disappointments in my encounter with Barth. But if extreme fundamentalists think I am going to join their "holy war" against Barth, they are sadly mistaken. I am convinced that Barth is an inconsistent evangelical rather than an inconsistent liberal. I base this conviction on two separate observations. First, whoever gives the *Church Dogmatics* a careful and fair reading will recognize that Barth has risen to classical stature on such matters as the trinity, justification by faith, the person and work of Christ, and critical implications of the gospel touching both the Christian community and general society. I concur with the estimate of Barth voiced by Professor Jaroslav Pelikan, the skillful moderator of the panel, when he said that for many years he had been teaching about church fathers but had never before known one personally.

Second, whatever Barth may lack in the way of doctrinal consistency he compensates for by his Christian graciousness. There was nothing affected about him; it seemed obvious that he lives by the grace that he preaches. Commented one of the journalists attending the lectures: "Merely to watch Karl Barth walk into the auditorium is a religious experience." I agree.

When I said good-by to Professor Barth for the last time he put an arm around me and asked if I were satisfied with the answers he had given to my questions. I thanked him for even considering them. I also thanked him for the Christian quality of his life as shown to us during the week. My debt to him is beyond repayment.

Part Two
On Paul Tillich

Paul Tillich has synthesized German speculation and American pragmatism. Depth psychology, with its roots in the Viennese school, is the key to this synthesis. Freud recovered the symbolism of common grace by accepting people who were unacceptable. Grace communicates a sense of worth. "You cannot help people who are in psychosomatic distress by telling them what to do. You can help them only be giving them something — by accepting them."

Within this pragmatic climate Tillich dilates the more speculative aspects of his system. Christology, for example, answers to man's search for self-realization. "There is a power from beyond existence which for us is verifiable by participation. This gives

Part Two published originally as a review of Tillich's book, *Theology of Culture*, in the July 6, 1959 issue of *Christianity Today*. Reprinted by permission.

quite a different type of Christology. Christ is the place where the New Reality is completely manifest because in him every moment, the anxiety of finitude and the existential conflicts are overcome. That is his divinity." To separate the threads of biblical truth from this skein of speculative error will require considerable patience and theological skill.

Tillich evacuates Scripture of its dogmatic rights by contending that philosophy enjoys autonomy in "the description of the structures and categories of being itself and of the *logos* in which being becomes manifest. Any interference of theology with these tasks of philosophy and science is destructive for theology itself." One could only wish that the matter were this easy. Tillich, it would seem, has made an unfortunate concession to worldly wisdom.

Relieved of dogmatic theology, Tillich seldom misses a chance to depress those elements in Scripture that fall outside his system. The account of the virgin birth, for example, is "a most obviously legendary story, unknown to Paul and to John. It is a late creation, trying to make understandable the full possession of the divine Spirit of Jesus of Nazareth." This hypothesis may be fashionable in critical circles, but it is void of accuracy.[1] If we neglect the historical elements in Christianity out of a zeal to defend the transcendent elements, we exhibit a very poor understanding of Christianity.

When we ask Tillich why he builds his system on those parts of Scripture that he himself considers important, he replies in a somewhat disarming tone. First, he takes refuge in Protestant liberty. "There is no pope in Protestantism, and if the Bible speaks, it speaks to *us*. Not only is there no pope, there is no council of bishops, no presbyters, no voting of church members on these matters." Second, he appeals to the way in which the church has conducted itself in previous cultures. Culture, he believes, dictates the church's attitude toward the gospel.

> Easter is by far the most important festival of the Russian church. In the medieval church, it was the anxiety resulting from the social and spiritual chaos following the breakup of the Roman Empire which produced the transcendent-sacramental foundation of a hierarchical system to guide society and individuals. In the Reformation it was the anxiety of guilt and the message of justification which was decisive for every formula of all the Reformers.

[1] The historicity of this event is brilliantly defended in J. Gresham Machen's *The Virgin Birth of Christ* (New York, Harper, 1930).

> In modern Protestantism it has been the message of a religious cultural unity in view of a more personalistic — and in America, more social — conception of the Kingdom of God as a religious cultural unity.

For the benefit of readers who are nervously waiting to learn whether Tillich is propagating heresy, a consolatory announcement can be made with dispatch. By no stretch of Christian charity can Tillich's theology be considered consistently biblical.

When we place Tillich on the Index, however, have we really accomplished anything constructive? Hardly. Christ did not shed His blood so that we might spend our days as spiritual vultures, feeding on the carrion of other people's shortcomings.

The fact remains, and no orthodox remonstrance can change a line of it, that cultured people will continue to read Tillich — and with no small profit. Tillich, for example, defines sin as estrangement — "estrangement from oneself, from the otherman, from the ground out of which we come and to which we go." At first blush this seems to contradict the confessional definition of sin as "any want of conformity unto, or transgression of, the law of God." But it may turn out, on more careful inspection, that the two definitions are quite friendly. Estrangement is a want of fellowship, and a want of fellowship is sin. Love is the law of life.

Although Tillich prefers speculation to exegesis, he yet is one of the most stimulating thinkers of our day. He is energetically trying to make faith relevant. And that is more than can be said of many who boast possession of the divine oracles.

Tillich challenges culture on the analogy between the gift of God's grace and the expression of kindness in therapeutic psychology. God accepts people who are unacceptable.

> This, of course, includes the reformation point of view, a view which has also been rediscovered by medicine, namely, you must feel that you have been accepted. Only then can one accept himself. It is never the other way around. That was the plight of Luther in his struggle against the distorted late Roman Church which wanted "that men make themselves first acceptable and then God would accept them." But it is always the other way around. First you must be accepted. Then you can accept yourself, and that means, you can be healed.

The church has been culpably tardy in applying Freudian insights to the biblical doctrines of original sin, common grace, and justification.

Since confessional Christianity tends to be anachronous in its thought forms, Tillich may seem more radical than he really is.

In any event, Tillich is here to stay. Even if a critic rejects everything Tillich says — an almost impossible situation — Tillich will nonetheless force the critic to do some very serious searching of soul. And who knows what may come of this? For if the critic were to show a little more concern for Tillich's truth, Tillich might show a little more concern for Tillich's error.

Part Three
On Orthodox Judaism

Many people picture orthodox Jews as an eccentric society, bearded, with their backs to progress and their faces to the Wailing Wall. Herman Wouk pictures them as a religious aristocracy commissioned by God to bear the torch of piety and learning until the very end of time. The darkest hours of Jewish persecution are turned into the brightness of meridian sunlight. The law of Moses "prophesied that the glories would be temporary, that the people in their prosperity would lose their hold on the law and on their land, and would scatter into exile; and it ordained that the nation should go on observing the festivals wherever they dwelt, to all time. And so we do. Our people have lived for thousands of years in the faith that in God's good time He will restore the nation to its soil, and that the festivals will take on, in the latter days, their ancient force and beauty" (Herman Wouk, *This Is My God*, p. 80). It is striking that Protestant dispensationalism would heartily agree with this interpretation of Israel's future.

Wouk is really trying to persuade "assimilated Jews" that a dissolution of Jewish distinctives would be a catastrophe. "We are nothing at all, or we are a people apart, marked by history for a fate embracing the heights and the depths of the human experience" (p. 283). It is only by courtesy that Christians are allowed to overhear this solemn conversation.

Christians who listen carefully may be surprised by what they hear. Wouk not only defends the divine authority of the Mosaic law, but he supports his defense by a dexterous use of religious symbolism, logic, moral institution, and the latest discoveries of archaeology. His command of Jewish sources is impressive, but he never overwhelms the mind with a cascade of sheer information. He writes with an authentic sense of dedication.

Part Three originally published in the Nov. 23, 1959 issue of *Christianity Today* as a review of Herman Wouk's book, *This Is My God*. Reprinted by permission.

If Christians think that orthodox Jews are on the verge of a great evangelical awakening, they are indulging in wishful thinking. With the founding of Israel as a state, orthodox Jews are all the more persuaded that God has destined them to remain a distinct people forever. "... I believe the survival of the Jewish people looks like the hand of Providence in History .... I believe it is our lot to live and to serve in our old identity, until the promised day when the Lord will be one and his name one in all the earth" (p. 20). This view of Providence is rather like that of Roman Catholicism.

After Christians manage to catch their breath, they may rightly inquire how orthodox Jews can rest their hope on a law that was designed as an instrument of death, not life. Wouk gives us the answer, though not by design.

Modern Jews take refuge in the same chambers of authority that sheltered the chief priests and Pharisees in the days of Jesus Christ. Judaism credits Moses with supreme authority, but in practice it vests this authority in the common law as set forth in the Talmud and later commentaries on the Torah. "Moses in his wisdom marked off only a few things in life that would endure. The rest he left to change. He did not freeze Jewish manners for all time in the cast of Egypt or of the desert" (p. 234). The elders of Israel may amend the law to meet the needs of the times and the abilities of the people. "The enabling clause for amendment is a passage in Deuteronomy which instructs Israel to abide by the Torah as taught to them by their sages" (p. 202).

According to the New Testament, the purpose of the law is to reveal man's wretched estate, that man may turn to God for grace and forgiveness. Wouk gives the impression that keeping the law is really not an unpleasant thing at all. If the Jews were to turn aside from the law, they would forfeit the happy calendar of ceremonies that gives depth to the religious year.

The gospel is the good news that God put the curse of the law on His Son, Jesus Christ. Orthodox Jews void the gospel by evacuating the law of its severity. The law is reduced to a manageable code of conduct. This code serves as a status symbol for a people who reject Christ's messianic claims, but who suffer no twinges of remorse for doing so.

This raises a very disconcerting point. The Apostle Paul says that "salvation has come to the Gentiles, so as to make Israel jealous" (Rom. 11:11). Now, just how jealous are orthodox Jews? If Wouk represents their attitudes correctly, they are not jealous at all. In fact, their cup is full and running over. Thunders Wouk: "What is absurd in Judaism? The Torah is there. Its heroes are human. Its history is accurate. Its religious imagery is immortal. Its disciplines are understandable. Moses is as persuasive a lawgiver as any that ever lived. The Prophets are apostles of the social justice that the whole world seeks today. Is it absurd to look for God? It is just as absurd not to look for him, life today being what it is" (p. 337).

Another thing: orthodox Jews have a long memory. They recall the dreadful anti-Semitic movements that have grown on Christian soil. These movements persuade Jews that Christianity is a sect which has lost the true glory of God by separating from the traditions of the elders.

Nor is this the end of the matter. When a student of church history compares the sweet fellowship of the primitive church with later religious wars and institutional struggles for primacy, he does not need a great deal of discernment to understand why orthodox Jews are not jealous of the Christian church. Gentiles are all too quick to charge Jews with clannish mannerisms, compromising business practices, and odd religious ceremonies. These charges root the Jews all the more deeply in their own traditions.

The issue remains the same today as it did in the time of the apostles. Did Moses look to the coming of Jesus Christ, or did he not? Christians say he did. "Do not think that I shall accuse you to the Father; it is Moses who accuses you, on whom you set your hope. If you believed Moses, you would believe me, for he wrote of me" (John 5:45-46).

This book has humbled my own heart, for I must confess that Wouk has done a remarkable job in defending orthodox Judaism. I wish I knew Wouk personally. He must be a pleasant man to be around.

I guess this leaves only one thing to be said. When orthodox Jews manage to outlive and outthink orthodox Christians, we need not be surprised if Israel continues to set her hope on the traditions of the elders and not on Jesus Christ.

CHAPTER FOURTEEN

The Government of the Church

As in other matters pertaining to faith and practice, the evangelical looks to Scripture when he defines the boundaries of acceptable church government. At first glance, however, Scripture seems disturbingly indecisive, for *specific* government is legislated for the church. The general principles of polity are clear, but not the details. This is one reason why questions of government have caused such deep and lasting divisions in the church.

It seems that the Spirit of God has been pleased to allow a certain flexibility in matters of form and order. In any case, we have no right to boast, for no branch of Christendom has precisely the same kind of government as that which existed in the early church.

I

The Necessity of Government

According to the Apostles' Creed, the church is a communion of the saints. This view comports with Scripture. True believers are a fellowship in Christ. This fellowship is not an external society whose rights dissolve when the corporation dissolves; it can exist without any organization at all.

But if this be true, why should the church be yoked with ecclesiastical rule? Why not let the fellowship carry itself? The answer is that government keeps the affairs of the church decent and orderly, in order that the ministry of the Word might not be hindered.

Although the church is not an external society, it is a vital society with a normative ground of existence. Christ is the head of the church, and Christ is confronted in and through Scripture.

Originally published in the June 22, 1962 issue of *Christianity Today*. Reprinted by permission.

This is why the ministry of the Word is so essential to the fellowship. Unless Scripture is studied and preached with diligence, Christians will not know what God requires of them.

But if the ministry of the Word is to prosper, it must be delivered from the distractions of secondary duties. Hence, the Lord has been pleased to ordain auxiliary ministries in the church — those of serving, teaching, and rule. These ministries, taken together, form the substance of church government. They give stability to the fellowship.

II
The Ministry of Serving

Scripture tells us that the ministry of serving was created to resolve a conflict of interests in the church (Acts 6:1-6). The Hellenists murmured against the Hebrews because their widows were neglected in the daily distribution. Charges of injustice threatened the fellowship. The apostles knew that something had to be done about the matter, and done at once. But they also knew that it would be wrong for them to leave the ministry of the Word to serve tables. Therefore, deacons were appointed to oversee the practical affairs of the church. *Nothing* must come between a pastor and his task of preaching the gospel.

There is no limit to the ways in which the ministry of serving can lift burdens from the ministry of the Word. When a pastor is cumbered by much serving, he neglects his duties as a shepherd of the flock. Rather than giving himself to prayer and meditation, he types stencils for the bulletin, does janitorial work, or coaches a basketball team. Or his strength may be depleted by larger distractions such as fund raising, building church properties, or managing a complex educational system. A pastor must follow the example of the apostles: he must practice the art of delegation. Christian education directors and psychiatrists may be as necessary to the ministry of serving in the modern church as deacons were in the early church.

III
The Ministry of Teaching and Rule

Although the apostles entrusted the ministry of teaching and rule to elders, the appointment of elders — unlike that of deacons — did not arise out of a specific incident in the life of the fellowship.

We are not told *when* the first elders were set apart or *why*. We are simply told that when relief was sent to the distressed brethren in Judaea, the money was delivered to the elders by the hands of Barnabas and Saul (Acts 11:29, 30). It appears that the office of elder belonged to the government of the church from the earliest times.

When Christ founded the church, He drew on a fellowship that was already in existence. This fellowship was formed of Israelites who were accustomed to the mode of government that prevailed in the synagogue. Therefore, it was only natural that this mode would be carried into the new communion. The office of elder "continued in substance what it had been hitherto under the Jewish synagogue system in its best days, with suitable modification and developments in accordance with the free spirit of the Gospel, and the Providential circumstances in which the Christian congregations found themselves placed. This presumption is confirmed by all the evidence, direct and indirect, bearing upon the point in the New Testament documents which belong to this period of history."[1]

Although the apostles outranked the elders in authority, the elders were destined to become the highest permanent officers in the church. There is no record that the office of apostle continued after the death of John; Scripture neither commands such a continuance nor does it specify the qualifications of those who should seek the office.

But the qualifications of those who seek the office of elder (or bishop) are specifically set down in Scripture (I Tim. 3:1-7). The question was not left to chance. The Apostle Paul appointed elders in the places where he had preached, and at great personal risk. We could ask for no more forceful proof that the Gentile churches were to be governed by the same polity that prevailed in Jewish churches.

IV

The Purpose of Elders

The elders were entrusted with the tasks of teaching and rule. "This double function appears in Paul's expression 'pastors and teachers,' where, as the form of the original seems to show, the two words describe the same office under different aspects. Though *government* was probably the first conception of the office, yet

[1]D. D. Bannerman, *The Scripture Doctrine of the Church* (Grand Rapids, Eerdmans, 1955), p. 410.

the work of *teaching* must have fallen to the presbyters from the very first and have assumed greater prominence as time went on."[2] The ministry of teaching and rule had exactly the same goal as the ministry of serving: to keep the affairs of the church decent and orderly, that the ministry of the Word might not be hindered.

After the elders were appointed by apostles, they served as a self-acting body. They could take the needed steps, with the concurrence of the congregation, to add to their number or to create any subordinate offices that might be needed for the more perfect life of the church.

It should be observed, however, that though the elders were to teach and rule, Scripture does not spell out their specific duties. Scripture assumes, as it does in the case of the deacons, that as long as the elders are full of the Spirit and wisdom, they will not only see what is required of them but they will discharge their duties with cheerfulness and dispatch.

V

The Functional Element in Church Government

The church is presently divided on whether the ministry of rule requires a separate officer, such as a bishop or superintendent, or whether this ministry belongs to pastors or elders who enjoy parity of rank. Two points should be noted in this connection.

First, the New Testament equates the offices of "elder" and "bishop." Therefore, any distinction between these officers is based on expedience, not principle. "There was in apostolic times no distinction between elders (presbyters) and bishops such as we find from the second century onwards: the leaders of the Ephesian church are indiscriminately described as elders, bishops (i.e. superintendents) and shepherds (or pastors)."[3] The validity of this exegesis is generally acknowledged.

Second, and more important, the ministry of rule, like other auxiliary ministries in the church, is free to develop its office according to the needs of the times. In the actual life of the fellowship, therefore, divergent modes of government may emerge. These modes may be the result of rich cultural and social influences. Or they may simply grow out of the dictates of expediency.

There may be times when a fellowship is so small that all the prescribed ministries in the church — that of the Word, serving,

[2] J. B. Lightfoot, "The Christian Ministry," in *Saint Paul's Epistle to the Philippians* (New York, Macmillan, 1896), p. 194.

[3] F. F. Bruce, *The Book of the Acts* (Grand Rapids, Eerdmans, 1954), p. 415.

teaching, and rule — may devolve on the pastor himself. As he succeeds in training others, he can delegate the auxiliary ministries. But he must proceed slowly, for it is not wise to lay on hands hastily (I Tim. 5:22).

When a fellowship reaches vast proportions, however, expedience may dictate that a separate office of rule be created. And it makes precious little difference what name is given to the officer in charge — whether bishop, archbishop, superintendent, or stated secretary.

In some cases it may be more expedient to vest the office of rule in a group of men — a council of pastors or elders, a pastor and his deacons, or the like. Neither the number of men nor their title is important. The important thing is that the office of rule is founded on biblical principles.

VI
Church Discipline

When church members are guilty of gross immorality, they must be excluded from the fellowship until they give signs of evangelical repentance. The New Testament is clear at this point (see for example I Cor. 5). Gross immorality cannot be ignored; and neither can it be tried by just anybody. If the fellowship is to be kept decent and orderly, specific persons must be vested with authority to administer discipline. Spheres of lawful jurisdiction must be defined.

When church members follow false teaching, however, the New Testament is not so clear. On the one hand, Christians are commanded to continue in the teaching of Christ and the apostles. But on the other hand, they are not told precisely what doctrines are essential to fellowship, nor are they told precisely what to do with errorists. For example, certain Judaizers went about teaching the necessity of circumcision (Acts 15:1-5). The apostles denounced the error, but they did not excommunicate the Judaizers. Again, there were some in Corinth who denied the resurrection (I Cor. 15:12). The Apostle Paul was shocked by such a denial, but he did not command the Corinthians to undertake heresy proceedings. And so it goes (see, e.g., Rom. 16:17; II Thess. 3:14, 15; I Tim. 6:3-5; II Tim. 2:14-19; Titus 3:9-11; and II John 9-11).

Since the data in the New Testament are not decisive, it is only natural that the church will be divided on how far to go when confronting errorists with the evil of their ways. Some denominations will create elaborate judicial machinery, while others will try to exclude errorists by the use of moral pressures alone. The mechanics of discipline are not important. The important thing is that the church is sincerely trying to continue in the teaching of Christ and the apostles. Complacency and indifference are the attitudes most to be feared.

VII
Conclusion

Since church government is a servant of the fellowship, it is a means and not an end. This is an important point. We must not separate from one another because we do not agree in details of government. If we do, we forget that love, not skill in ecclesiastical rule, is the sign of a true disciple. Worldwide Christian fellowship is the ideal for the church. Whatever hinders this ideal should be brought under the scrutiny of the Scriptures.

Instead of boasting about superior polity, we ought to occupy ourselves with the weightier matters of the law — justice and mercy and faith. "Happier are they whom the Lord when he cometh, shall find doing in these things, than disputing about 'doctors, elders, and deacons.' "[4]

Devising new offices is not the whole answer to problems arising out of the complexity of the modern church. The offices in the New Testament are simple and effective. The sheer multiplying of offices may be a sign that the church is substituting human wisdom for a life of faith and grace.

We do not need additional officers as such. What we need is prophets of God who can call existing officers back to biblical standards. As long as rulers are filled with the Spirit and wisdom, *any* form of government will do. And if rulers lack these virtues, even the most cleverly devised polity will be found wanting.

Too much government leads to tyranny, whereas too little government leads to anarchy. Either extreme disrupts the fellowship. Good rulers will not only steer the course between these extremes, but they will cheerfully acknowledge that their own authority is derivative and subordinate. Ecclesiastical rule has no independent rights. It exists as a handmaid to the ministry of the Word.

[4] Richard Hooker, *Of the Laws of Ecclesiastical Polity* (1890 ed., reproduced photographically by the Univ. of Chicago Press), Preface VI, 5.

CHAPTER FIFTEEN

The Case for Orthodox Theology

Part One

Orthodoxy does not have all the answers; nor does it always ask the right questions. And when it gives the right answers to the right questions, it often corrupts its claims with bad manners.

But beneath these outer garments is the warm flesh of Christian truth: the truth that love is the law of life; that all men are sinners; that Christ bore the penalty of sin; that repentant sinners are clothed with the righteousness of Christ; that Christ is confronted in and through the written Word; and that the Word is consistent with itself and with the things signified.

We have defined orthodoxy as "that branch of Christendom which limits the ground of religious authority to the Bible." The testimony of Christ is normative for the church, and included in this testimony is the assurance that the written Word is inspired of God, and that it has the force of law.

Orthodoxy is often branded as literalism. The charge is that orthodoxy defends the plenary inspiration of the Bible, even though destructive criticism has ostensibly demolished this doctrine. But it is instructive to note that the critics seldom give a precise definition of literalism; nor do they go on to tell what *they* mean by the Bible as the Word of God. If orthodoxy neglects destructive criticism out of a respect for the testimony of Christ, the critics neglect the testimony of Christ out of a respect for destructive criticism. Not only is the neglect mutual, but it is by no means clear that the neglect of the critics is more praiseworthy, let alone more Christian, than that of orthodoxy.

If we nullify the testimony of Christ at one point, we operate on a principle that leaves the mind free to nullify this testimony

Part One originally published as the last chapter of Carnell's book, *The Case for Orthodox Theology*, copyright© 1959 by W. L. Jenkins, The Westminster Press. Used by permission. The work appeared in a trilogy with *The Case for Theology in Liberal Perspective* and *The Case for a New Reformation Theology*, by others.

at all points. In this case we have little reason to believe that our hope rests on divinely appointed evidences — not even our hope that God sent His Son to be the Saviour of the world. The evidences that support the plan of salvation are precisely the same in quantity and quality as those which support the plenary inspiration of the Bible.

If orthodoxy is literalistic because it honors the rights of language in Scripture, it is in very good company, for Christ and the apostles approach the text in precisely the same manner. Critical reinterpretation may relieve faith of the scandal of plenary inspiration, but it also relieves faith of the scandal of the cross. Tested by the canons of science and philosophy, the doctrine of justification fares no better than the doctrine of plenary inspiration.

When the gospel is absorbed into a world system, the minister can no longer stand behind the sacred desk and cry, "Thus says the Lord!" And when the voice of the prophet is silenced, let "Ichabod" be written over the church: the glory has departed.

The cause of destructive criticism cannot be rescued by contending that revelation is personal encounter with Christ, and that this encounter is valid whether or not the Bible is inspired. Not only is the contention void of proof, but it reduces Christian commitment to a variety of religious experience. By no analysis of personal confrontation could we discover that God made a covenant with Abraham, and that Jesus Christ is the blessing of this covenant. Only propositional revelation can clarify the state of a sinner before a holy God.

Christ taught that the plan of salvation was mediated to the church through the office of inspired prophets and apostles. If we reject this office, we forfeit the norm by which the limits of valid confrontation are decided. In this case the religious experience of an animist has the same rights as that of a Christian, for neither the animist nor the Christian has any proof that his faith terminates in the mind of God. Religion becomes an exercise in personal feeling.

Critics also brand orthodoxy as fundamentalism, but in doing so they act in bad taste. Not only is it unfair to identify a position with its worst elements, but the critics of fundamentalism often manifest the very attitudes they are trying to expose. The mentality of fundamentalism is by no means an exclusive property of orthodoxy. Its attitudes are found in *every* branch of Christendom: the quest for negative status, the elevation of minor issues to a place of major importance, the use of social mores as a norm of virtue, the toleration of one's own prejudices but not the prejudices of others, the confusion of the church with a denomination, and the avoidance of prophetic scrutiny by using the Word of God as an instrument of self-security but not self-criticism.

The mentality of fundamentalism comes into being whenever a believer is unwilling to trace the effects of original sin in his own life. And where is the believer who is wholly delivered from this habit? This is why no one understands fundamentalism until he understands the degree to which he himself is tinctured by the attitudes of fundamentalism.

Critics have not performed their full task until they leave the externals of orthodoxy and probe into the heart of the system itself. And once this nobler task has been executed, the critics may discover that orthodoxy is a worthy Christian option. In any case, the problems of orthodoxy are common to all who try to discover the essence of Christianity and to live by its precepts.

In the sweep of history it may turn out that orthodoxy will fail in its vocation. But in this event it should be observed that it is orthodoxy, not the gospel, that has failed. The Word of God is *not* voided by the frailties of those who come in the name of the Word of God.

Part Two

Since contributing to this trilogy on Protestant theology, I have engaged in some serious searching of soul on the meaning of the Protestant principle, and especially on the manner in which this principle connects with the normative elements in Christian theology.

The Protestant principle came into being during the celebrated Leipzig Disputation of 1519. Luther was goaded, step by step, into contending that the Council of Constance erred in condemning Hus. On hearing this contention, Eck leaped to his feet and thundered, "*Heretic*!" Luther was a heretic, and thus a Protestant, because he dared to test the traditions of Roman Catholicism by Scripture and right reason.

I know how it feels to be branded a heretic by Rome, for during graduate studies I tried to enter into theological conversation with several Jesuit priests. All went well until I challenged their exegesis. They answered, with flashing eyes, that they were under sacred vows not to consider the possibility of truth outside their

Part Two originally published in the October 1959 issue of *The Journal of Bible and Religion* as a review of the other two books in the Westminster Trilogy.

own papal traditions. I told them, in parting, that I had a better chance of finding truth than they did, for unlike them I was free to consider both sides of a question. My remark made little impression.

A Protestant has a sacred duty to test theology by Scripture and right reason, for theologians are sinners, and sinners are prompted by interest as well as truth. We somewhat obscure Christianity in our very effort to clarify Christianity. Hence, we must submit our partial insights to the communion of the saints. And we must do this not once or twice, but again and again, until we walk by sight and not by faith. Free and open conversation is the very lifeline of Protestant theology.

In reflecting on the parts of this trilogy, I am convinced that each author has done his best to square theology with the claims of right reason. In no case has faith become an excuse for intellectual laziness.

But I do not believe that an equal effort has been made to square theology with the claims of Scripture. It is here, not on the issue of right reason, that Protestant theology divides into such elements as orthodoxy, liberalism, and neo-orthodoxy.

It seems to me that if Protestant conversation is to be fruitful, a really dedicated effort must be made to recover the Reformation view of religious authority. Luther overturned the medieval synthesis in confidence that the Holy Spirit inspired holy apostles to found and instruct the church. It was only as Luther liberated the Pauline doctrine of law and grace that a genuine criterion of debate emerged.

Luther defended revelation as a disclosure of the divine person. Indeed. But Luther also defended revelation as a disclosure of the divine will. He experienced forgiveness of sins by personal confrontation with Christ; but he drew the normative elements of his theology from propositional revelation.

Orthodoxy feels that both liberalism and neo-orthodoxy depreciate the normative elements in theology: liberalism, out of a zeal for humanistic creativity; neo-orthodoxy, out of a zeal for revelation as a disclosure of the divine person. It is an exegetical fact, and no remonstrance against orthodoxy can change a line of it, that apostles were appointed to render a normative interpretation of the redemptive events. "And God has appointed in the church first apostles . . ." (I Cor. 12:28). The apostles were chosen by Christ; they were first eyewitnesses, then preachers of Christ's resurrection; their gifts were excellent and extraordinary; they were endowed with the spirit of prophecy; and they enjoyed primacy over the entire church.

Roman Catholicism contends, of course, that if the apostles bequeathed a normative interpretation, it is fatuous and inept to say we must continue to correct our theology by free and open conversation. Since we have the truth, let us submit to it, not search for it.

Rome neglects one very stubborn fact. Even though the apostles render a normative interpretation of the redemptive events, we still have to *interpret* this interpretation. Before we can submit to the apostles, we must use our own judgment to decide what the apostles said. And despite the most painstaking efforts, our theology will always be one step removed from the precision of the apostles. Protestant divines are not blessed with the gift of inspiration, and neither are the divines of Rome. Luther quite successfully proved that Roman Catholic theology is an interpretation of what the apostles said, and at many points a very poor interpretation at that.

Liberalism and neo-orthodoxy dismiss orthodoxy as dogmatic and outmoded, and in so doing think they end the issue of apostolic authority. This optimism is wide of the mark. Let us remember that the Protestant principle came into being by a *recovery*, not a *denial*, of the normative elements in Christian theology.

If we depreciate the authority of the apostles, we not only offend the communion of the saints, but we also offend a rule that cultured people have honored since Plato demolished the man-measure theory in the *Theaetetus*; the rule, namely, that whenever a difference of opinion arises about the meaning of specific data, the novice should defer to the judgment of the expert. When judging histology, a physician is more qualified than a shoemaker; and when judging theology, the apostles are more qualified than modern theologians. We are separated from the redemptive events by nearly two thousand years.

Liberalism and neo-orthodoxy will reply, of course, that the apostles do more than witness to Christ's life, death, and resurrection. They also speak of such time-bound matters as baptism for the dead, decorous female attire, and whether a man should give his virgin in marriage. From this and similar evidence, it would seem that we must subordinate the apostles to standards drawn from human wisdom.

I do not think a genuine difficulty is here being raised, and the Reformation is proof of it. There is no cause to go beyond the apostles, provided we use a little horse sense when defining our rules of hermeneutics. The apostles supply a criterion by which we can distinguish between the permanent and temporary elements in the apostolic witness. Luther knew this, and so did the other Reformers. There are places in the New Testament where the apostles develop doctrine in systematic, didactic language. These places serve as a criterion by which the force of everything else in Scripture is decided. Protestants should remember that it was only after Luther recovered the theology of Romans and Galatians that an understanding of the Bible, as the cradle of Christ, took shape. Spiritual confrontation is nurtured by propositional revelation, not the other way around.

I do not say that Protestants should suspend conversation until they agree on the exact nature of apostolic authority. I only say that Protestants will never get on with it unless they acknowledge, in good faith, that the apostles knew a lot more about Christian theology than we do. Only a pompous egotist would put his judgment on a par with that of Peter and Paul.

Protestants must recover the Reformation balance between revelation as a disclosure of God's *person* and revelation as a disclosure of God's *will*. The first is mystical and inward; the second, objective and propositional. If we drive a wedge between personal and propositional revelation, we evacuate Christian theology of its normative elements. In this event, our conversation about faith reduces to an exercise in aesthetics. We may say we have been confronted by Christ, even as a Christian Scientist may say he has been confronted by Mary Baker Eddy, but no soteric expectations can be grounded on this sort of evidence.

Let me give the pith and marrow of what I am trying to say. If Protestants fail to distinguish between apostolic testimony and their own interpretation of this testimony, they corrupt the Protestant principle by slighting the threshold of variable error that attends all biblical exegesis. They return to the ethos of Roman Catholicism. But if Protestants make this distinction, and yet refuse to improve their interpretation by submitting to apostolic testimony, they corrupt the Protestant principle by making themselves equal with the apostles. They repudiate the normative elements in Christian theology. The first error overlooks the work of sin in theological inquiry; the second, the authority of the apostles in detecting and correcting this work. If orthodoxy tends to make the first error, liberalism and neo-orthodoxy tend to make the second. At least this is the way it seems to me.

CHAPTER SIXTEEN

The Fear of Death and the Hope of the Resurrection

Illness is an evil because it saps our strength. It leaves us damaged, like a wormy apple or a chipped vase. When we are ill, we are not the self we wish to be. We cannot do the things we want, and there is so much we really want to do .... When we become ill, some part of our body is failing us; and when an important part fails we die, that is all. Even a headache is advance warning that death is on the way ....

We may delay death by prudence and circumspection. But we cannot keep death from reaching us in the end. Death's knock may be gentle at first, very deceiving, as of a friend who awaits us. But soon the knock will become rude and insistent. Then we shall have to open the door, whether by day or by night.

Some people are so afraid of death that they will not even talk about the grave. They do not avoid dying, but they think they have a better time living. They might have an even better time if they drew their wits about them and faced up to the limits God has placed on the creation ....

The fear of death draws many people near to God. As they sense their own weakness, they long for resources that only God can give. They believe that by surrendering themselves to God, things will work out happily in the end. God will not forsake His friends. But the fear of death also separates many from God. They are disturbed by the problem of evil.

I

In an atomic age we must learn to live with the threat of imminent death. At first glance it may seem that our predicament has no new elements in it. But this is not quite accurate. Our forefathers granted that life ends in death, but they viewed death as a *distant* foe. Now the foe is near at hand.

In the pre-atomic ages there was always the possibility — if we may compare life to an ocean voyage — that the ship might flounder on hidden reefs or be swamped by a storm or be plundered by pirates. But the voyage was reasonably safe, for the threat of imminent death was relieved by knowledge that the ship was sound, the course well plotted and the powder dry. In an atomic age we face identical perils. But we are no longer able to relieve the threat of imminent death, for we have discovered to our dismay that the ship itself is not seaworthy, that we may be sent to a watery grave at any moment. Thus the blue expanse which once calmed our anxious souls has become an agent of terror.

Psychologists have amassed an impressive body of evidence to prove that Christians often suffer from a fear of death, and that on this particular question they in no way differ from men in general. If this is the case, with what right do Christians continue to say that God has delivered them from a fear of death?

This is no mere academic issue, nor am I dealing with cold statistics. For despite my Christian background I myself am now and then seized by feelings of consternation and alarm. Frankly, I am terrified when I am told that everything we hold dear can be reduced to atomic ashes the moment a few military men push a few buttons. This terror not only unmasks my great affection for the things of this world but makes me seriously wonder how my life differs from that of the naturalist who repudiates the idea that man is made in the image of God, and who derives no comfort from the hope of immortality.

Whenever I fall into seasons of depression a cloud of futility hovers over my soul. I keep asking myself what is the point of writing books or teaching seminary students when our very way of life is suspended over the abyss of nothingness. Nor do I feel relief when I recall that soldiers often become better men when they learn to live with the threat of imminent death; for soldiers are borne along by the consolation that after the strife of battle they will return to their homes. In the event of an atomic war we shall have no such consolation.

It is easy for self-righteous Christians to widen the gap between life and the church by boastfully contending that they transcend this whole problem. They open a copy of Scripture and read that Christ gave His life to "deliver all those who through fear of death were subject to lifelong bondage" (Heb. 2:15). Closing the sacred text and glancing up with an arrogance matching that of the doctors of the law in Christ's day, they find a certain delight in defending their own spiritual superiority. If a Christian happens to suffer from a fear of death, they imply, he is not much of a Christian.

These latter-day Pharisees conveniently overlook the manner in which Christ Himself faced the prospect of death. "When they reached a place called Gethsemane, he said to his disciples, 'Sit here while I pray.' And he took Peter and James and John with him. Horror and dismay came over him, and he said to them, 'My heart is ready to break with grief; stop here, and stay awake.' Then he went forward a little, threw himself on the ground, and prayed that, if it were possible, this hour might pass him by" (Mark 14:32-35, New English Bible). Of course, it would be easy to dismiss this passage by contending that Christ's fear was confined to His spiritual suffering as Saviour and that He had no more fear of physical death than did Socrates. But we dare not take it upon ourselves to separate the physical and spiritual elements in Christ's crucifixion. Moreover, Scripture plainly teaches that the Lord partook of flesh and blood, just as we do. And fear is an unavoidable aspect of finitude — at least in this present world.

A careful reading of the Bible shows that the feeling of depression has had a long history. The Psalmist cries: "Remember, O Lord, what the measure of life is, for what vanity thou hast created all the sons of men! What man can live and never see death? Who can deliver his soul from the power of Sheol?" (89:47-48). The author of Ecclesiastes goes so far as to claim that the dead are more fortunate than the living, and that the most fortunate one of all is he who has not been born (4:2-3). And so it goes.

Since repentance does not repeal the law of self-preservation, we should be neither surprised nor embarrassed when we find Scripture reviewing these symptoms of depression. A Christian is *nowhere* promised exemption from the law of self-preservation. If a Christian did not do his best to go on living, he might neglect his responsibility to serve as the salt of the earth. But God has checked this possibility by ordaining that the law of self-preservation should remain active unto the end. Hence we should not be disturbed when we learn that some Christians have a morbid fear of the grave. After all, we are entitled to seasons of depression if we are so inclined. God does not expect us to go about with a Cheshire-cat grin. "For he knows our frame; he remembers that we are dust" (Ps. 103:14).

It should be carefully noted, however, that after Christ poured out His soul in prayer He emerged from Gethsemane with a feeling of perfect peace. The transformation symbolizes the biblical promise that God *will* give us grace to pass through the valley and shadow of death. The experience of Samuel Johnson, whose wisdom was surpassed only by his piety, perfectly illustrates this truth. Throughout his life he suffered from a terrible fear of death. But when it came time for him to die God flooded his soul with grace. "We shall presently see," writes Boswell, "that when he approached nearer to his awful change, his mind became tranquil, and he exhibited as much fortitude as becomes a thinking man in that situation."

Thus when a Christian says he is free from the fear of death he means — or at least I think he *should* mean — that he is not afraid to meet his Maker. Having been reconciled to God through the blood of Jesus Christ, he senses a holy boldness to stand in the presence of God. "For God did not give us a spirit of timidity but a spirit of power and love and self-control" (II Tim. 1:7). If we are careful with our use of terms, we can confidently say that *no* true believer has a fear of death. Regardless of how desperately a Christian may cling to the things of this world, or of how often he may fall into depression, in his devotional self he grants that to die and be with the Lord is better.

Let us note in this connection that prison chaplains often find that inmates seek consolations which go beyond the grave and reach into the intimacies of the soul itself. "Thus conscience doth make cowards of us all," says Hamlet in his soliloquy. It is ironic, but a severely distressed person would likely be *relieved* if he could be sure that death would put an end to everything. The validity of this conjecture is illustrated by the behavior of the Nazi bigwigs at the Nuremberg trials. With the exception of the philosopher Alfred Rosenberg (who may have wept in his heart), all of them called for a priest or minister in order that they might render a good confession before going to the gallows. They could endure the agony of physical death, but they had no resources to meet God.

A hearty Yes and No may be the nearest a Christian can come to answering those who inquire whether he fears death. So long as the law of self-preservation remains active within us, we may experience times of depression similar to those recorded in Scripture. Therefore, if a Christian finds that he fears the threat of imminent death in an atomic age, he should not on that account feel guilty or unworthy. He is still a human being; he still clings to life—like everyone else. But at the same time he can forthrightly assert that he is not afraid to stand in the presence of God, for he has already made peace with God through the Lord Jesus Christ. A Christian may know little about the furniture of heaven, but he is sure of one thing, and this is all that matters: *God loves him.* "Beloved, we are God's children now; it does not yet appear what we shall be, but we know that when he appears we shall be like him, for we shall see him as he is" (I John 3:2).

Let us strive with all our might to persuade rulers and nations to enter into negotiations that will issue in a workable balance of power and a reasonable basis for peace. But if the threat of nuclear warfare continues to mount, let us remind ourselves that God is sovereign. He says to the nations, as He says to the tides of the sea: "Thus far shall you go, and no farther."

And if it is God's will that we must face apocalyptic times, let us calmly learn to say (despite the "other law" which wars against the law of the mind): "I have been crucified with Christ; it is no longer I who live, but Christ who lives in me; and the life I now live in the flesh I live by faith in the Son of God, who loved me and gave himself for me" (Gal. 2:20). As the Apostle Paul noted long ago, whether we live or die we are the Lord's. What more could the heart desire?

II

Call it folly, call it wishful thinking: the fact remains that no upright person can believe that his loved ones are only animals that perish. The intellect may accept the gloom of the grave, but the intellect is not authorized to speak for the heart. The heart draws on convictions that are foolishness to both science and philosophy. An upright person knows that if the departed do not count, then the living do not count, for the living and the departed are inseparably joined by the bond of love....

When the Apostle Paul preached in Athens, his audience

listened until he spoke of the resurrection. "Now when they heard of the resurrection of the dead, some mocked; but others said, 'We will hear you again about this' " (Acts 17:32). It is ironic that the Greeks were offended by the very doctrine that evokes the highest feelings of joy in Christians. Paul was so certain of his ground that he linked the very hope of mankind to the resurrection of Christ. "Now if Christ is preached as raised from the dead, how can some of you say that there is no resurrection of the dead? But if there is no resurrection of the dead, then Christ has not been raised; if Christ has not been raised, then our preaching is in vain and your faith is in vain" (I Cor. 15:12-14). Christ's resurrection is proof that the Father received the sacrifice of the Son. All who are in Christ will be raised in like manner, for Christ is the firstfruits from the dead.

The Greeks wanted eternal life, but they saw little point to the resurrection of the body. Since the real man is the rational man, the body is an extraneous element. And even worse, it is a positive hindrance to man's unclouded vision of truth. We are saved by being divested of body, not by being reunited to body. Socrates drank the hemlock on the confidence that he would soon be liberated from his corporeal prison . . . .

Martha, the sister of Lazarus, rested in the Semitic conviction that man is a vital union of body and soul. If you take away the body, you take away an essential part of man. This is why the hope of eternal life was eventually linked with the hope of the resurrection.

The Semites not only enjoyed the light of special revelation but they came at the issue by way of the convictions of the heart. Thus, when Martha tried to picture Lazarus in the kingdom of heaven, she could only picture him as she knew him in Bethany. If he did not have a body like unto the one that she remembered, he would not be the same person . . . .

Since all observable evidence supports the conclusion that man perishes at death, the resurrection of the body is as offensive to science as it is to philosophy. And when Christians speak of a *spiritual* body, critics say that the end of good sense has come.

But the Apostle Paul thought otherwise. In fact, he went to considerable pains to tell just what the resurrection body would be like. It would belong to a new order of physics. "What is sown is perishable, what is raised is imperishable. It is sown in dishonor, it is raised in glory. It is sown in weakness, it is raised in power. It is sown a physical body, it is raised a spiritual body" (I Cor. 15:42-43). But how did Paul expect cultured people to believe this? The answer is, he told them to behold the risen Lord. Jesus was raised from the dead, and His body was spiritual in substance. He not only ate fish with His disciples, but He passed through closed doors. Therefore, as Paul saw the issue, Jesus' resurrection body proved that God not only *could* create a new order of physics, but that He actually *did.* Reality itself sets the limits to possibility.

Paul was fully convinced that Jesus was raised from the dead. The evidences were sufficient, for Jesus "appeared to Cephas, then to the twelve. Then he appeared to more than five hundred brethren at one time, most of whom are still alive, though some have fallen asleep. Then he appeared to James, then to all the apostles. Last of all, as to one untimely born, he appeared also to me" (I Cor. 15: 5-8).

The Greeks groaned under the limitations that sin places on our present bodies. This is why they wanted to be emancipated. They knew that the body is subject to passions that war against the soul.

But since the Greeks did not have the light of special revelation, they did not know that the resurrection body will be divested of sin. When man is confirmed in righteousness, the conflict between soul and body will cease. The body will become a servant of the soul.

III

Scoffers dismiss the hope of heaven as an innocent but fruitless projection of wishful thinking. They grant that it would be *nice* to believe that good people have nothing to fear, but where is the evidence for this belief? Jesus has come and gone, and things continue as they were from the beginning. Nature is a conflict between regular and irregular forces, society a conflict between justice and injustice. Therefore, would it not be better, let alone more honest, to make this world a happier place in which to live, rather than selfishly dreaming about heaven?

Indeed, we *should* do all we can to make this world a happier place in which to live, for love is dedicated to the task of relieving suffering. But unless love is joined by faith and hope, it cannot complete its mission. Love is an eternal tie; it draws on consolations that reach beyond the grave. Love says to the beloved, "You have nothing to fear, now or at any other time." Hence, the hope of heaven is not a sign of selfishness. It is a sign that love is being true to its own essence.

Jesus does not distribute photographs of heaven, nor does He satisfy the standards of science and philosophy. But He does satisfy the convictions of the heart, and He satisfies them with the highest of all possible evidences. Jesus *promises* an eternal home to all who trust Him. What more could be asked?

Since the law of sin is actively at work in our members, we often promise more than we can make good. But Jesus faces no such prospect, for He is one in nature with the Father and the Holy Spirit. By His own resurrection from the grave He proved that He is Lord of the new creation .... Christians do not know why God was pleased to create a world into which such frightful things as illness and death should come. But they do know that God never intended to let illness and death have the last word. And they know this because God has declared Himself in the person of Jesus Christ.

When we become discouraged by the evils of the day, let us remember that Jesus gave His life with the express purpose of leading many sons into glory. As long as we are good, the evils of the day cannot harm us.

Science and philosophy will continue to boast of awesome achievements, but these achievements will neither add to nor subtract from the pleasure that a believer feels when God says, "I accept you: you count in my sight." Since our lives are hid with Christ in God, we have a reason for living and a reason for dying. "So we do not lose heart. Though our outer nature is wasting away, our inner nature is being renewed every day. For this slight momentary affliction is preparing for us an eternal weight of glory beyond all comparison" (I Cor. 4:16-17) ....

Every beat of the heart bears witness to our finitude. We are *not* the authors of our own existence. All our striving will prove futile in the end. Death will overtake us; our bodies will become food for worms.

This is why we must set our hope on God alone. When we are joined to Christ through faith and repentance, we are justified before the law and adopted into the family of God. The Lord then tells us that death is only a chamber in which we lay aside our earthly tabernacle with its pains and hindrances.

We were alone when we entered the world, but when we leave it we shall feel the abiding presence of the Lord. As death draws near and we dread the dark journey ahead, the Lord will assure us that our lives are precious in the sight of God. He will gently say, "Child, come home." Jesus has given His word that He will never leave us nor forsake us, and His word is as firm as His character.

"Therefore, my beloved brethren, be steadfast, immovable, always abounding in the work of the Lord, knowing that in the Lord your labor is not in vain" (I Cor. 15:58).

Bibliography of Books and Articles by Edward John Carnell

Books

1948-*An Introduction to Christian Apologetics* (Grand Rapids, Eerdmans).

1950-*Television: Servant or Master?* (Grand Rapids, Eerdmans).

1951-*The Theology of Reinhold Niebuhr* (Grand Rapids, Eerdmans).

1952-*A Philosophy of the Christian Religion* (Grand Rapids, Eerdmans).

1957-*Christian Commitment: An Apologetic* (New York, Macmillan).

1959-*The Case for Orthodox Theology* (Philadelphia, Westminster).

1960-*The Kingdom of Love and the Pride of Life* (Grand Rapids, Eerdmans).

1965-*The Burdenof Søren Kierkegaard* (Grand Rapids, Eerdmans).

Articles

1948-"Why Neo-Orthodoxy?" *The Watchman-Examiner,* Feb. 19, 1948.

1948-"Is Drunkenness a Sin?" *United Evangelical Action,* Mar. 1, 1948. (Reprinted in *The Union Signal,* May 15, 1948.)

1950-"How Every Christian Can Defend His Faith," *Moody Monthly,* January 1950 (Part I); Feb. 1950 (II); Mar. 1950 (III).

1950-"The Problem of Religious Authority," *His,* Feb. 1950.

1950-"The Christian and Television," *His,* May, 1950.

1951-"Should a Christian Go to War?" *His,* April, 1951.

1951-"The Grave Peril of Provincializing Jesus," *The Pulpit,* May, 1951. (Reprinted in *The Presbyterian Outlook,* Mar. 31, 1952.)

1951-"Beware of the 'New Deism,' " *His,* December, 1951.

1956-"Niebuhr's Criteria of Verification" (Chapter 18), in *Reinhold Niebuhr: His Religious, Social, and Political Thought,* ed. Charles W. Kegley and Robert W. Bretall (New York, Macmillan).

1956-"A Proposal to Reinhold Niebuhr," *The Christian Century,* October 17, 1956.

1957-"Reinhold Niebuhr's View of Scripture" (Chapter 9), in *Inspiration and Interpretation*, ed. John W. Walvoord (Grand Rapids, Eerdmans).

1957-"The Nature of the Unity We Seek: An Orthodox Protestant View," in *Religion in Life*, Spring, 1957. (Reprinted as "Orthodoxy and Ecumenism" in *Christianity Today*, Sept. 1, 1958.)

1957-"Can Billy Graham Slay the Giant," in *Christianity Today*, May 13, 1957.

1957-"Billy Graham and the Pope's Legions." Editorial in *Christianity Today*, July 22, 1957.

1957-"Personal Happiness and Prosperity," *Christian Economics*, Sept. 3, 1957.

1958-"Fundamentalism," in *A Handbook of Christian Theology*, ed. Marvin Halverson and Arthur A. Cohen (Cleveland, World).

1959-"The Third Day: Jesus and the Multitudes," across top of Part 3, *Los Angeles Times*, Mar. 24, 1959.

1959-"The Case for Orthodox Theology" (excerpt from book of same title), in *Christianity Today*, April 27, 1959.

1959-"Post-Fundamentalist Faith," *The Christian Century*, Aug. 26, 1959.

1959-Essay on "A Trilogy of Protestant Theology," in *The Journal of Bible and Religion*, Oct. 1959.

1959-"The Virgin Birth of Christ," in *Christianity Today*, Dec. 7, 1959.

1960-Articles on "Thomism," "Existentialism," "Immaculate Conception," "Perpetual Virginity," "Reatus Culpae, Reatus Poenae" in *Baker's Dictionary of Theology*, ed. Everett F. Harrison, Geoffrey W. Bromiley, and Carl F. H. Henry (Grand Rapids, Baker).

1960-"Orthodoxy: Cultic vs. Classical," in *The Christian Century*, March 30, 1960.

1960-"Jesus Christ and Man's Condition," in *Encounter*, Winter 1960.

1960-"Evil-Why?" (reprinted from *The Kingdom of Love and the Pride of Life*), in *Eternity*, Dec. 1960.

1961-"Capital Punishment and the Bible," in *Eternity*, June 1961.

1961-"The Secret of Loving Your Neighbor," in *Eternity*, July 1961.

1961-Reprint of "Orthodoxy: Cultic vs. Classical" in *How My Mind Has Changed* (Cleveland, World).

1962-"Barth as Inconsistent Evangelical," in *The Christian Century*, June 6, 1962.

1962-"The Government of the Church," in *Christianity Today*, June 22, 1962. Reprinted in *Basic Christian Doctrines*, ed. Carl F. H. Henry (New York, Holt, Rinehart and Winston, 1962).

1963-"The Fear of Death," in *The Christian Century*, Jan. 30, 1963.

1963-"A Christian Social Ethic," in *The Christian Century*, Aug. 7, 1963.

1965-"Conservatives and Liberals Do Not Need Each Other," in *Christianity Today*, May 21, 1965.

Book Reviews

1950-Review of Alan Richardson, *The Gospel and Modern Thought,* in *The Westminster Theological Journal,* Nov. 1950.

1954-Review of J. M. Spier, *Christianity and Existentialism,* in *The Westminster Theological Journal,* May 1954.

1956-Review of Cornelius Van Til, *The Defense of the Faith,* in *The Christian Century,* Jan. 4, 1956.

1956-Review of George Hendry, *The Holy Spirit in Christian Theology,* in *The Christian Century,* Nov. 21, 1956.

1957-Review of Baillie, *The Theology of the Sacraments,* in *Eternity,* Aug. 1957.

1958-Review of Karl Barth, *The Word of God and the Word of Man,* in *Eternity,* 1958.

1958-Review of Richard R. Niebuhr, *Resurrection and Historical Reason,* in *The Gordon Review,* Summer 1958.

1959-Review of Reinhold Niebuhr, *Pious and Secular America,* in *Eternity,* Feb. 1959.

1959-Review of Henry Zylstra, *Testament of Vision,* in *Religion in Life,* Spring 1959.

1959-Review of Paul Tillich, *Theology of Culture,* in *Christianity Today,* July 6, 1959.

1959-Review of Herman Wouk, *This Is My God,* in *Christianity Today,* July 6, 1959.

1959-Review of Robert Clyde Johnson, *Authority in Protestant Theology,* in *The Christian Century,* Dec. 16, 1959.

1960-Review of Jean-Paul Sartre, *The Devil and the Good Lord,* in *Christianity Today,* July 6, 1960.

1960-Review of *Baker's Dictionary of Theology,* in *Christian Herald,* July 1960.

1960-Review of Aldert Van Der Zeil, *The Natural Sciences and the Christian Message,* in *Christianity Today,* July 18, 1960.

1960-Review of Gordon Harland, *The Thought of Reinhold Niebuhr,* in *Christianity Today,* Aug. 1, 1960.

1960-Review of Nels F. S. Ferré, *Know Your Faith,* in *Christianity Today,* Aug. 29, 1960.

1960-Review of Chang Chen-Chi, *The Practice of Zen,* in *Christianity Today,* Oct. 10, 1960.

1960-Review of W. Norman Pittenger, *The Word Incarnate,* in *Christianity Today,* Nov. 7, 1960.

1961-Review of H. Richard Niebuhr, *Radical Monotheism and Western Culture,* in *Christianity Today,* Jan. 30, 1961.

1961-Review of Otto A. Piper, *The Biblical View of Sex and Marriage,* in *Christianity Today,* Feb. 13, 1961.

1961-Review of Robert McAfee Brown, *The Spirit of Protestantism,* in *Christianity Today,* June 5, 1961.

1961-Review of Nels F. S. Ferré, *Searchlights on Contemporary Theology,* in *Christianity Today,* July 3, 1961.

1965-Review of Harold Lindsell (ed.), *Harper Study Bible,* in *Christianity Today,* Feb. 12, 1965.

1965-Review of Oliver J. Buswell, Jr., *Systematic Theology of the Christian Religion,* in *Christianity Today,* Feb. 26, 1965.

1965-Review of James O. Overholser, *A Contemporary Christian Philosophy of Religion,* in *Christianity Today,* May 7, 1965.

1966-Review of *New Directions in Theology Today,* Vols. I and II, in *Christianity Today,* Nov. 25, 1966.

Unpublished Dissertations

1948-"The Concept of Dialectic in the Theology of Reinhold Niebuhr," Th.D., Harvard Divinity School.

1949-"The Problem of Verification in Søren Kierkegaard," Ph.D., Boston University.

Studies of Carnell's Thought

Barnhart, J. E. *The Religious Epistemology and Theodicy of Edward John Carnell and Edgar Sheffield Brightman.* (Unpublished Ph.D. dissertation, Boston University, 1964.)

Nash, Ronald H. *The New Evangelicalism* (Grand Rapids, Zondervan, 1963).

Ramm, Bernard. *Types of Apologetic Systems,* first ed. (Wheaton, Van Kampen, 1953).

Sailer, William S. *The Role of Reason in the Theologies of Nels Ferre and Edward John Carnell.* (Unpublished S.T.D. dissertation, Temple University, 1964.)

HIEBERT LIBRARY
3 6877 00203 2182